THE GARDENER'S
GUIDE
TO
BETTER SOIL

BY
GENE LOGSDON
AND THE EDITORS OF
ORGANIC GARDENING
AND FARMING

Rodale Press, Inc.
Emmaus, Pennsylvania 18049

Printed in the United States of America

Fourth Printing (pbk.) — April 1978
407

Library of Congress Cataloging in Publication Data
Logsdon, Gene.
    The gardener's guide to better soil.

    Includes bibliographical references and
index.
    1. Soil science. 2. Organic gardening.
3. Soils—United States. I. Organic
gardening and farming. II. Title.
S591.L57   631.4   75-33191
ISBN 0-87857-106-X
ISBN 0-87857-117-5 pbk.

Contents

Chapter

Contents

Contents

Chapter 1

You're a Very Important Person on Earth

Plowing my little field for corn last spring, I learned anew the importance of organic matter in the soil. The land at one end of the field was hard, yellow clay—marble ground I call it—while the rest of the field was rich, black loam, full of humus. Pulling the plow through the hard clay, the tractor would groan almost to a halt and I'd have to shift down to a lower gear. The soil slithered off the moldboards of the plow in greasy, shiny slabs. A potter's dream perhaps, but a nightmare to a farmer. What I was plowing was subsoil bared to sun and rain by years of erosion. Nothing much was going to grow in that humus-starved clay. It was fit only for buckwheat, which will send its tough roots through almost any kind of soil and loosen it. As it now lay, the dirt would work down to a seedbed of small rock-hard clods or dust. Rain, even just a shower, would hit it and run off rather than soak in. The sun would then bake the wet surface into a cement-like crust through which germinating seeds could barely push, if at all. There was no joy in plowing such land.

1

Halfway back across the field, the tractor seemed almost to sigh with relief as the plow slid into the good, black loam. Now the earth tumbled over the moldboards and flowed out behind so soft and crumbly that you could hardly tell one furrow from the other. Here was soil to build a civilization on! Such earth could produce a crop at much less expense to an energy-short nation. For instance, I could immediately shift into a higher gear—drive faster without increasing fuel consumption. Working this plowed ground into a seedbed with disk and harrow would take only half as much fuel and energy as the hard clay would. In fact, I could scatter seed carelessly on such humus-rich ground and it would grow without any seedbed preparation at all. Rain, even a downpour, would neither crust this land nor run off, causing erosion. The USDA says that land with more than 4 percent humus content will soak up a six-inch rain before there is any runoff.

Another farmer, walking across the field, picked up a handful of that black loam and let it slide out between his fingers. "If all the land were like this, wouldn't farming be paradise," he said.

It would. In fact, if every human being would keep just one acre in that condition, or put one acre into that condition, the whole world would be much closer to paradise. At least I can think of a whole lot of problems, of which food shortages are just one, that would dissolve before our eyes—if for no other reason, a lot of people would be too busy to get into much mischief. I recommend the project as a full-time occupation for about a third of the people in Washington D.C.

Soil and Food

The purpose of this book is to tell you how to make your plot of garden or fields as fertile as that loam, so that you can raise an abundance of food naturally—with very little dependence on costly outside supplies of fossil energy. I don't know which of those two goals—enriching the soil or raising the food—you consider more important, but it makes little difference. In accomplishing the first goal organically, you achieve the second automatically. But it isn't easy. Especially in the beginning. You will need all the motivation you can get, which is the reason I want to tell you *why* making good soil is as important as *how* to make it. I want to convince you that organic gardeners and farmers are very important people to have around. If your gravestone could read, "Here lies a person who left his land with over 5 percent organic matter in it," you could rest assured that you had contributed as much good to the earth as any famed scientist, philosopher, or philanthropist. Maybe more. And in the bargain, you would have achieved a sort of immortality. For your children's children and their offspring will see in their day, when the supply of life's necessities is really critical, the importance of organic matter in the soil and they will revere the memory of those people who are now trying to halt man's careless waste of such a vital natural resource.

Soil and Civilization

The much-admired soil scientist George Scarseth, now deceased, used to tell his students that if man took care of the top seven inches of the earth's crust, just about everything else would take care of itself. Other agriculturists put it a slightly different way: "Man is only seven inches from starvation"—the seven inches or so of topsoil from which we all, in one way or another, derive our sustenance. Neither of these remarks is just an attempt to be cute, or to oversimplify, or to make idle poesy. The fall of almost every civilization is largely an account of raping natural resources until all the easy profit goes out of them. This has been pointed out by historians so often it hardly seems worthwhile to give examples again. All you have to do is read what the ancient Roman naturalist Pliny wrote about the agricultural splendors of the Tigris and Euphrates valleys. Then go to Iraq today and compare. On most of the land in those valleys now you could not raise an umbrella if you stood on a sack of fertilizer. The same for parts of Iran, Lebanon, the valley of the Nile, and much of China, though the latter is painfully trying to renew its agricultural productivity. Wherever a dense population of that greedy primate, man, has lived the longest, you will find the rape of nature the most severe. Painful as it is to say it, man is the earth's number one problem.

But we are not intentionally vicious in our wasteful ways. Scarcity slips up on us by such small degrees that one hardly recognizes it in the span of a mere generation or two. Man finds good land and establishes a "civilization." His flocks graze the grass; he tills the soil. He waxes fat and sassy and multiplies in number. Increased populations put more demand on the productive capacity of his land. Overgrazing and over-tilling both follow. Plant life becomes too weak to restore itself, and the soil grows yearly more deficient in plant food and tilth. Weak plants can't control erosion. As Scarseth would say, rain and wind do not cause farm erosion, lack of nitrogen and organic matter do. Deforestation, overgrazing, intensive tillage all then contribute to a hard soil where water runs off quickly. Summer soils become annually drier and winter floods more destructive. Water supplies cease to be dependable year around. Before every civilization begins to falter, it engages in a couple of centuries of massive irrigation projects to store water and put it back on the land. Having denuded the land so that it would not hold water, it then must store the water running off and put it back on. If the process sounds a little insane, you have grasped the problem.

Farming Out America

You don't have to hark back to some ancient civilization to see what happens. Just take a close look at the United States. The "civilized" human race took from the Indians the richest, most expansive chunk of farmland in the world. We mined out the native fertility of that ground in a century. It is no mystery why the nineteenth century was least concerned with famine in all history. We were eating literally off the fat of the land in America. It solved Europe's immediate problem too. Europe could stabilize the depletion of its soils, which had been going on at a rapid rate during the eighteenth century, by shipping its excess population to the United States. (Cuba has been doing the same thing over the last 15 years.)

By 1930 we had farmed the easy living out of America. Even senators were impressed when the dust from Oklahoma windstorms blew all the way to Washington D.C. Soil conservation went into high gear. The first Soil Conservation Service survey in 1933 revealed that things were in pretty bad shape—over a billion acres showing harmful, man-caused erosion, with 100 million acres so badly eroded as to be ruined for farming. Moreover, thousands of acres of grasslands in the semiarid Great Plains were either overgrazed or broken to the plow, eventually causing the kind of duster that ripped through western Kansas on May 11, 1934. That storm carried away an estimated 300 million tons of topsoil, enough to clothe 3,000, one-hundred-acre farms with a sufficient covering of good dirt.[1]

Technology

Once alarmed, Americans brought technology to the rescue. On thousands of farms, soil conservation practices were put into effect: dams, grass waterways, contoured slopes, chisel plowing, terraces. More significantly, we began to use chemical fertilizers in awesome amounts, while hand-in-hand we manufactured farm machinery that could handle awesome numbers of acres in a day. Both the fertilizer and the machines used up awesome amounts of fossil fuel and other resources, but at the time no one thought we were robbing Peter to pay Paul.

By the middle '60s technology seemed to have ended any fear of famine forever. In fact, our problem was huge surpluses of food. Agribusiness and the agricultural press bragged that American farmers alone could feed the whole world. Soil and water conservation became such a passé subject that the Soil Conservation Service could begin building big lakes for urban recreation on the best river bottom land we had.

Today it appears almost certain that while technology was providing us with an extravagance of plenty, it was not solving the problem but only staving it off. Take those lakes the Soil Conservation Service and the Army Corps of Engineers were building. In Iowa, just to mention one state, the engineers were surprised when at least three of the huge water impoundments built there silted up with eroded soil so badly within a few years after they were built that they are now barely suitable even for boating, fishing, and swimming!

The area that showed the greatest increase in agricultural production during the '60s was the Great Plains, as increasing population pushed farms out of more amenable land in the eastern half of the country. Why could the Plains produce so much food? Irrigation. Huge irrigation rigs now water 160 acres in a few hours. Underground water is being pumped from the soil at such an alarming rate that stiff regulations are needed in the Southwest to ration the amount each user takes. Some of this water, especially in Texas and parts of Oklahoma and Kansas, is fossil water. It comes from underground lakes that are not replenished. When it's gone, it's gone. In other states, especially Nebraska, the supply of underground water is "unlimited." This is the favorite adjective on the tongues of irrigation equipment makers, Nebraska bankers, and Nebraska farmers, all of whom proudly—and justifiably—point to the economic rebirth of hundreds of small towns in the state directly caused by irrigation farming.

Unlimited? Every intelligent man knows that is wishful thinking. The forests were unlimited too. Such resources are unlimited only if they are used wisely, and man has not shown much aptitude for wisdom. Now that its economy is built on irrigation, what will eastern Nebraska do if its wells run dry?

In the '70s, we know that such questions are not stupid. Nitrogen is "unlimited" too, so why couldn't farmers get enough of it in the spring of 1974 for their crops? Because nitrogen, *in the form modern agriculture has committed itself to use,* is a by-product of the fossil fuel industry. Our mineral or fossil sources of phosphorus and potash are now "ample," but they are not "unlimited." Phosphoric acid can be derived from animal bones, and as such is a renewable source, but a meager one. Some day we may have to derive phosphoric acid from human bones, which certainly makes more sense than entombing them in a satin-lined box. Potash occurs in small amounts in many plant fibers, especially wood, and in manures. It occurs in some organic mineralized deposits too, but these should be mothered carefully and used sparingly just as our phosphate rock deposits.

A New Agriculture

The '70s have brought us face to face with the limits of a technology that assumes unlimited natural resources. In the case of agriculture, the energy crisis has inadvertently revealed a new and extremely important value of organic gardening and farming—a system which provides food without the total reliance on fossil energy that is agriculture's burden today.

The technology that can make this new system work is being crafted by trial and error in organic gardens and on small organic farms today. And you are the researcher in charge. The open-minded members of the scientific establishment are taking another look at organic, natural agriculture. They may have scorned earlier organic declarations that certain manufactured chemicals are harmful and unnecessary in raising food, but they know, as you know, that a self-renewing agriculture depends upon a rich content of organic matter in the soil. And the energy crisis has made them realize that the artificial means they have brainwashed farmers and gardeners into using as substitutes for high organic matter content are going to become too scarce or costly to depend on.

Food producers are feeling the pinch already. This spring (1975), as I write this, I have just visited with two neighboring farmers. The first is today's typical farmer. He is planting corn. But even though he made a lot of money last year, he is not as optimistic as he usually is at spring planting time. The reason is that he will have spent around $150 *per acre* on that corn crop, mostly on chemicals, before it is knee high. By the time he harvests it, his costs will be well over $200 per acre— an all-time historical high. All this is money regardless of his yield or his market price. His yields probably will not be up to expectation because he could not afford enough artificial nitrogen (even if available) that he had been taught to use to get that yield. The same industry that had lured him to total dependence on inorganic fertilizer had backed out on supplying him totally, and to add insult to injury, made him pay nearly black market prices for what he did get. Farmers have traded their independence for the vision of a Florida vacation.

Down the road from this fellow lives Farmer Number 2. Farmer No. 2 is known in the county as a little on the radical side. Weird. He doesn't use chemical fertilizer. Or herbicides. Or bug killers. He just pours up to twenty tons of manure per acre on his land plus eight dollars worth of a soil amendment that has a guaranteed analysis of 0-2-2. All right—thinking men around him declare that eight dollars for something like that is just thrown away, but they never question any part of the six times that amount they pay for chemical fertilizers. You might think they would when they saw Farmer No. 2's corn produce over 100 bushels per acre last year, though planted a month late. Or his hay, which produced over eight tons per acre (he says ten tons but I don't believe it). What is Farmer No. 2's secret? *The organic matter level in his best fields is now up to a phenomenal 4.9 percent,* and I *do* believe that because that analysis comes from Brookside Laboratories, an independent firm I have great respect for. What is even more surprising is that Farmer No. 2's farm was poor, rundown land ten years ago, with the organic matter content 1.8 percent. You don't change a farm like that to good soil by dreaming about Florida in winter. Fertilizer shortage? Farmer No. 2 isn't worried. "This isn't a showplace and I don't claim to have all my problems solved," he says. "But soil fertility isn't one of them."

Farming and the Gardener

The organicist is the scientist of this new agriculture and his garden is his laboratory. If the predicted critical food shortages are avoided, I think the credit will go to gardeners and small homestead farmers, who are now moving in unprecedented numbers to properties large

9

enough to enable them to raise some of their own food. Homesteaders have decided that independence, satisfaction, and the economic savings derived from raising their own food are important enough to bend their energies to the task. Government may tell us how much of our money we can keep, but it is not going to tell us how much we can or cannot eat—even Russia found that out. When we are told that there is a shortage of wheat, or that milk will go to more than two dollars a gallon, or that good meat may become too costly to produce, somehow we know we're being played for suckers.

Enough of us can feed ourselves to make the difference between feast and famine in the years ahead. All any homeowner needs is a half acre or more and *knowledge*—the kind of knowledge commercial agriculture has received from years of tax-funded research. The making of food is one craft that is accomplished better as a cottage industry anyway, and the sooner we bend technology to shape a viable cottage-industry agriculture, the better. If our agricultural colleges are so financially tied to agribusiness that they cannot help bend the technology our way, we will do it ourselves.

The job can be done, and this book is written for those who want to do it. We will learn how to take care of our soil . . . and our soil will take care of us.

Chapter 2

Getting Acquainted with Your Soil

If you've ever driven on a long trip (or even a short one) with a couple of gardeners in the car, you know who enjoys travelling more than most people. To anyone sensitive to soil and green growing things, a stretch of lonely highway or a nondescript little village becomes a scene of high adventure. Where there are two gardeners in the car, the conversation usually goes like this:

"Hold it, Joe. Back up. Did you ever see such a neat garden? Look at that soil—black as the ace of spades."

"If I had soil like *that* I could grow ten pound cabbages, easy."

"What kind of tree is that blooming over there, Betty?"

"It looks like a walnut tree to me, and they only grow on good soil."

"That's folklore. The sign of good soil is where burdock grows."

"Burdock growing in a garden is a sign of a lazy gardener."

"Now look up there on that hill. Look at that erosion. You know, you could probably stop that by throwing five handfuls of grass seed over there in the spring."

"Trees. I say plant all hills to trees."

"Hey, there's a goldfinch. Why can't we get goldfinches in our garden?"

"Over there's a smart farmer. He's growing clover. I think I'm going to try that in the garden. Nothing like clover for a green manure crop."

"Joe, if you don't watch where you're driving, the only gardening you're going to be doing is pushing up daisies."

A Soilwatching Trip

So the talk goes for miles and miles, each garden and farm passed becoming a chance for the "soil-watcher" to collect a new type of soil the way bird-watchers collect birds. It's a game you can learn to play too with profit for your own gardening projects. A trip from New Jersey to Chicago, for instance, could acquaint you with a very wide variety of soils even if you never got out of the car. If you know how to read the signs, those soils can tell you interesting stories as you drive along.

Pine Barren Sand

The best time for soilwatching from the highway is April, May, and June when farmers are cultivating and planting. If you start in central New Jersey, the first soil you "collect" will be the most bizarre of all—pine barren sand, one of the few sandy soils that is rich in organic matter. It is also very acid (pH 4-5) and so uniquely qualified for growing blueberries, cranberries, and other acid-loving plants. The white sand in the barrens becomes brown sand outside the barrens, and the brown is not so endowed with organic matter. Irrigated and limed to lessen acidity, it produces good vegetable crops. But let drought, or even just a week of dry weather come, and plants like corn on unirrigated land begin to wither. Nowhere can you get a better lesson in the importance of organic matter.

Two Red Soils

Driving into Pennsylvania north of Philadelphia you can take the Northeast extension of the Pennsylvania Turnpike towards Allentown and see two more fairly unusual soils, a red podzol soil (most reds are laterites) and a light grayish, extremely gravelly soil. On the latter, potatoes are grown chiefly. The gravelly soil *looks,* to an oldtime cornbelter like me, to be poor and highly erosive, but actually it is neither. It erodes, of course, as any soil on steep slopes will, but not nearly as much as one would suspect of such a gravelly soil.

On the other hand, the red soil, a clay, does erode badly, a characteristic you can observe when a field of it is planted to wheat. Wheat is planted much the way you would plant grass, and it generally forms a "sod" which controls erosion fairly well. But not so well on this red clay.

The red soil looks poor too, but originally it was the best land in the area. Old farmers between Allentown and Lansdale will tell you that farming the red soil often brought wealth after several generations of good farmers, while farming on the gray-brown soils gave only a living at best. Careless farming on the red soil brought erosion, and now the red soil is even redder because more subsoil is mixed into it. In some places all that is left is subsoil, and on it only poverty grass and cedar trees will grow well. You can see a nice stand of cedar trees at the Lansdale exit of the Turnpike.

The major portion of the red soil area is now being developed for houses, and as you drive along you will notice that the bulldozer boys have learned nothing from the farmers who first mistreated this ground. They shove the red earth into shapes according to their hearts' desires, and are surprised when one good rain carries half the dirt back into roads and ditches. Sometimes a month's expensive bulldozer work is ruined in one night's rain, not to mention ruin downstream from the tons of eroded dirt. Ask the people who live around Kulpsville, Pennsylvania, if you think I'm exaggerating.

No Topsoil

When you head west on the Turnpike, once beyond Philadelphia, you pass through Chester and Lancaster counties. Near Coatesville, Pennsylvania, a farmer rents land that has no topsoil on it at all—it has been stripped off for making mushroom soil. To make that subsoil produce 75 percent of what the topsoil would have grown, the farmer must dump tons of manure on it and lace it heavily with chemical fertilizers to boot. Only because he can rent the land for next to nothing can the farmer "break even" at all. The mushroom soil eventually can be returned to this land, so what happens to this soil is not quite a catastrophe. But it's a good example of the enormous expense involved in trying to produce food after the topsoil is gone. Anyone who has tried to make a garden on subsoil left by a builder around a new house understands this very well.

Limestone-Rich Loam

As you pass the Morgantown, New Holland, and Lancaster exits of the Turnpike, note well the gardens and farms in the neighborhoods. The limestone-rich loam you see is some of the richest soil in the world. In a sense, if a real food shortage develops, every use of that land except food-raising would be a mistake we might not be able to afford.

Not only is this a naturally fertile soil, but much of

it has been nurtured and cared for by Amish and Mennonite farmers. Farms are remarkably small by American standards—modern agribusiness says a fifty-acre farm is too small to make a living on, but the Amish don't know that, so they go right on making a living, ofttimes becoming wealthy in the bargain. Their land is gently cared for because their agriculture emphasizes the raising of livestock, with home-grown grains fed to the animals and the manures and beddings returned to the land.

You need only to drive through the back roads of this region to know the soil is rich. Not only are crops lush, houses and barns neat and substantial, but small local industries thrive everywhere—always the case where agriculture is profitable. Farm and factory often coexist placidly side by side; village and pasture melt into one another. Parts of Lancaster County are living models of how to use land well for a total society. It all happened because the land was loved.

However, overpopulation is threatening to ruin Lancaster County farmland now. Good farmers are leaving, forced out by the taxes that come with population pressures. Drive through, and instead of gawking at the Amish men in their buggies like a bunch of New Yorkers, take a look at the last vestige of the golden era of agriculture in this country.

Rocky Soils

After you cross the Susquehanna River and pass the Harrisburg exits, you drive through an altogether different kind of country. Wide expanses of rather level land spread out on both sides of the road, running to the foot of honest-to-goodness mountains. Fields are bigger, slightly more level, tempting the use of the mammoth machines of modern agriculture. But this is not land that should be heavily cropped. For one thing, solid rock lies under a thin mantle of topsoil and here and there breaks

15

above the surface—breaking not only farm tools but farm bank accounts. This land can support prosperous dairies and other livestock enterprises that can make economic use of grass grazing on rocky soils. You can't see it from the road, but a few miles south and stretching on into Maryland, orchards have proven to be profitable too.

But you see a lot of deteriorating homesteads as well, homesteads that once were very profitable as the huge, unique, decorated-brick barns attest. But too many farmers decided to raise grains only and get rid of the livestock. When the livestock went down the road, so did the business—and the farmer's sons went with it.

Shale and Rock

Soon you are climbing over and tunneling through the mountains. Close up, the mountain-sides appear to be surfaced with pure shale and rock, and you wonder how the trees can grow there at all. But they do. No one knows exactly how beneficial those unending miles of forested mountainside are to man simply because he *can't* find any other use for them.

Stripped Land

In a few hours you pass through Wheeling, West Virginia, if you left the turnpike at New Stanton and proceeded straight west on Interstate 70. Then Ohio, and almost immediately, you are driving through strip-mined hills. Stop along the road and study some of the soil profiles, where the big coal shovels have gutted the land. You will be, or should be, surprised at how thin is the mantle of soil that covers this land. Mostly it is rock, but still, if you look toward the horizon, you see that the land can support forest and pasturage and even some cultivation. But know that you are looking at a basically poor farm land, not good land. Then consider that not more than twenty miles south of where you are parked along that highway lives one of the finest dairy-men in the country—and one of the best herds of cows. He did it on land only a little better than what the coal companies ruined in the past—land they liked to refer to as "marginal."

On the other hand, you can see along the highway you are travelling excellent examples of how coal com-panies have restored strip-mined land. Inspired laws and higher coal prices have forced or enabled (take your choice of verbs) the strippers to reclaim land they have pillaged, and they are doing a first-rate job of it. Much of their best reclamation in Ohio is right along Interstate 70, where all the world can see. (If you take the Fair-view exit and drive south you will see unreclaimed strip mines—the way the land is usually left after the coal has been taken out.) What the coal companies have demonstrated is that they can very often reshape the land after strip-mining so that it is better for grazing livestock and even raising grains than it was before. Looking at before and after photographs of reclaimed land is to glimpse a minor miracle. I don't mean to say that all the problems are solved (reclaimed land is highly erosive) but at least there is encouragement for any gardener who thinks *he* has a poor site for raising food.

Clay

Proceeding westward, you come to the Zanesville area and notice many signs beckoning you to pottery factories and retail pottery outlets—another use man makes of soil.

Just as certain types of sand in the soil around Wheeling brought a glass-making tradition to that area, so the clays of southeastern Ohio, centered in the Zanes-ville area, have long produced many types of earthen-ware. Pottery is probably the least important part of the industry; the clay also makes many kinds of drainage tile and wall tile for the building trade.

Prairie Soils

The closer you get to Columbus, the more level the land becomes, and you know from the lushness of the corn and soybeans and the size of the fields, which seem to stretch to the horizon, that you have entered the southeastern tip of the cornbelt. But the country is still broken by low hills and some rough land. Turn north at Columbus and in thirty more miles or so you really enter the "get big or get out" kind of farm country where corn, soybeans, and Florida is coming to be the usual rotation. Monstrous machines rule the land here as they do in the west, and if one chemical won't guarantee you a crop, there's two more that will. Of interest to the soilwatcher here is to note how the soil colors in any given field contrast between light and dark. The light soils are on the higher elevations, the black soil and the lower. Why? Years of farming have washed the original black topsoil off the higher ground.

As you look across such a field that is fairly level, the low-rising undulations of light soil look like splotches of sunlight through a buttermilk sky. In northern Illinois on similar terrain, the deeper prairie soils are black on the high ground too, and you don't get the effect you do here. Topsoils formed by forest decay are usually not as deep as those under prairie sods.

Farmers who still haul manure to their fields will generally put it on the high, poorer, light soils where there is little organic matter. With the advent of high-powered chemicals, farmers can shoot the juice to plants on this poorer soil and make them seem to grow as well as the plants on the black rich soil. But at great expense. How much more efficient and economical over the long haul to have kept the topsoil and the organic matter where it belonged.

From the standpoint of the gardener, it will make a great difference whether your vegetable plot can take advantage of the black soil, rather than be forced by circumstances of property lines to grow upon the light clay. Two suburban lots next to each other in a subdivision here could conceivably require quite different lawn and garden care.

Muck

In northern Ohio and lower Michigan you will meet yet another kind of soil—muck. Muck is proof that you can almost get too much of a good thing—organic matter. Mucks can contain 20 percent or more of organic matter. Such soil is black as coal, easily worked, level, soft, and springy. Dried out, muck soil will blow badly. But in dry weather, good crops can be raised on muck because almost always the water table is high under muck beds. But in a wet year, crops on muck often drown out. Onions are grown commercially on mucklands, and in Ohio, celery is a principal crop.

Mucks in some areas cannot be farmed or gardened until extensive drainage systems are built to lower the water table under them. But once dry, I've seen mucks catch fire and smolder deep in the ground for a year. About the only way to put out a muck fire is to flood the area over it with water—in other words, turn the spot back into a swamp the way it was before drainage.

Impermeable Clay

Heading west again towards Chicago, you will pass level tan soils in western Ohio, and some blackish soil that is extremely heavy with clay. Farming and gardening methods that rely on chemical fertilizers rather than organic matter make the soil so tight that water will not percolate down well enough to drain it with tile (a procedure described in Chapter 7). Excess water will lie on the surface almost as it will on cement. Surface drainage—shallow, graded ditching—is necessary to remove rainfall. Heavy as these clays are, they will grow excellent soybeans if handled correctly.

19

Prairie Loams

In western Indiana and on across north central Illinois, you pass through the deep, level prairie loams—black chernozem soils that are the heart and soul of the cornbelt. Some of this land, stretching on into Iowa, is covered with loess, a wonderful silt loam blown into thick topsoil deposits eons ago. On loess you could garden with no more tools than a dibble stick if you had to, and raise all the food you could eat.

Sandy Soils

If you continued your journey through central Wisconsin and on into Minnesota, you would observe soils where sand rather than clay is the major component, mostly brown sands in Wisconsin, blacker sands in Minnesota. The heavier sands make excellent garden soil; the lighter ones dry out and blow. This spring you could have watched sandy ground in central Wisconsin wind-drifting into piles along fence rows like snow in a blizzard. If you gardened here you would learn soon enough the miracles that organic matter could perform for such sandy soil—or you would learn to live with sand in your eyes like the farmers who insist on trying to cultivate this land as if it were good loam. Contrast the beautiful farmsteads and gardens of southern Wisconsin with the hardscrabble homesteads in the north. He who has eyes to see. . . .

Lessons of Soilwatching

Your trip, real or imaginary, should have taught you a few lessons:

1. Physical appearance of soil is not necessarily a good indicator of its value. A gravelly soil can be productive.

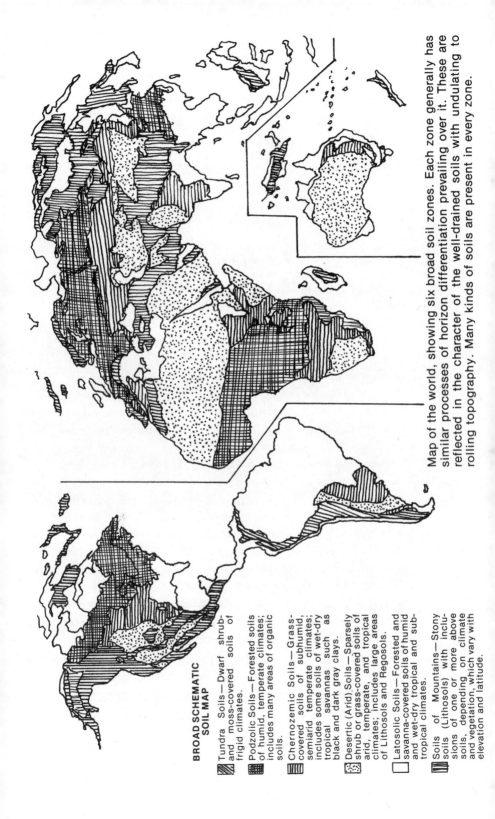

BROAD SCHEMATIC SOIL MAP

Tundra Soils—Dwarf shrub- and moss-covered soils of frigid climates.

Podzolic Soils—Forested soils of humid, temperate climates; includes many areas of organic soils.

Chernozemic Soils—Grass-covered soils of subhumid, semiarid temperate climates; includes some soils of wet-dry tropical savannas such as black and dark gray clays.

Desertic (Arid) Soils—Sparsely shrub or grass-covered soils of arid, temperate, and tropical climates; includes large areas of Lithosols and Regosols.

Latosolic Soils—Forested and savanna-covered soils of humid and wet-dry tropical and sub-tropical climates.

Soils of Mountains—Stony soils (Lithosols) with inclusions of one or more above soils, depending on climate and vegetation, which vary with elevation and latitude.

Map of the world, showing six broad soil zones. Each zone generally has similar processes of horizon differentiation prevailing over it. These are reflected in the character of the well-drained soils with undulating to rolling topography. Many kinds of soils are present in every zone.

2. Color is not an indication of fertility. A red soil may be as fertile as a brown or black.

3. Soil erosion is by far America's most dangerous pollutant.

4. Good places to garden are places where good gardens already exist. Ditto for farms.

5. Poor soil is five times more costly to farm or garden than good.

6. When industrial and population pressures force farmers off of good land onto poorer, a crime against wise land use has been committed.

Your trip should also have pointed out some basic soil differences and what the differences mean. Physically, soil can be sandy, gravelly, clayey, loamy, or mucky, with almost limitless combinations thereof. Tilth of any of these combinations is governed by the amount of organic matter—the more there is, the better the tilth. With respect to slope, the steeper the land, the more hazards involved in farming or gardening. In terms of moisture-holding capacity, soil varies from nil in pure sands to such a tightness in some clays that the land cannot be drained even with tiling. Measured by acidity, soil can have a pH as low as 3 (very acid) to as much as 8 (very alkaline), and the amount of acidity crucially determines what will and will not grow on a soil. Chemically, bacteria, microorganisms, and acids turn nitrogen, phosphoric acid, and potash from the minerals and organic matter at hand into food for plants. The soil also contains in varying amounts many other elements necessary for healthy plants, among which are iron, copper, manganese, calcium, zinc, molybdenum, and cobalt, to name a few. The interaction of all these ingredients in the teeming life of the soil is the essential activity of existence, but to a surprising degree, scientists don't know exactly how plants avail themselves of the nutrients that the soil's activity provides.

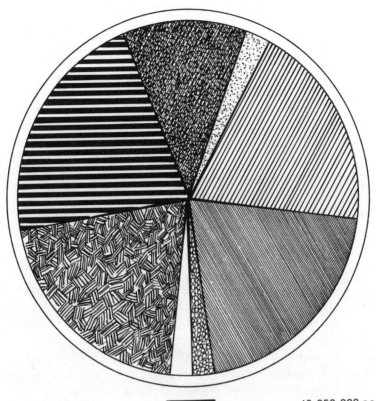

36, 174,000 acres 2 %	CLASS I 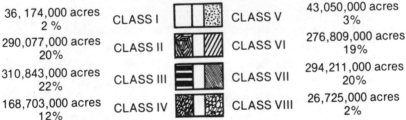 CLASS V	43,050,000 acres 3%
290,077,000 acres 20%	CLASS II CLASS VI	276,809,000 acres 19%
310,843,000 acres 22%	CLASS III CLASS VII	294,211,000 acres 20%
168,703,000 acres 12%	CLASS IV CLASS VIII	26,725,000 acres 2%

This pie graph shows the extent of land capability classes in mainland United States, according to the United States Department of Agriculture. The lands in Classes I, II and III are suitable for regular cultivation. Class IV lands are suitable for occasional cultivation, while Classes V through VIII contain lands not suitable for cultivation. There are about 1.5 million acres of unclassified lands.

The Perfect Garden Soil

A perfect soil for your garden would be a deep silt loam of good tilth, at least 5 percent humus, through which water percolates readily. It should contain 45 percent minerals, 25 percent water, and should be aerated well enough so that 25 percent of any given block of soil would be air space. If such soil had a pH of 6.5 to 7.0, had just been fertilized with about fifteen tons of rotted manure per acre, and had been dressed with a couple of tons per acre of rock phosphate two years ago, then you would have not just soil, but a priceless inheritance. On such land, you could as one gardener I know puts it, "stick a broom handle into the ground and it would grow."

Soil Maps

I have studiously avoided giving soils names. They do have names. They have so many names that not even an agronomist can remember half of them. Names of soils, like colors of soils, do not tell you much about how to garden on them. Most soils have been "mapped" —that is, the Soil Conservation Service has identified the soils of most of the counties of the states and located them on soil maps. That is how I know that the soil in the area of my homestead is a Blount-Toledo-Kibbie association, with a little Morley-Blount along the creek at the far end of the property.

But that means only that *generally* these particular soil combinations occur in the area. In any given spot within that area there could be (and in fact are) other soil types. What good does a *general* soils map do me, if my particular garden spot has another type? That's why, at least in Ohio, and I think elsewhere, the state Department of Natural Resources has now authorized a new and more detailed soil survey. Soon you'll be able to find out your garden soil's name with a glance at a map. That may not help you grow a better garden, but I suppose surveying soil is more productive work than giving political speeches or writing existentialist novels. Soil maps are at least helpful to big-shot housing and industrial developers who know nothing about an area where some corporation wants to build a subdivision or shopping center. Contractors and land buyers can look at the soil maps and avoid areas where, for instance, septic tank leach beds won't work. More to the point, a government agent can look at the maps and tell a contractor where he can build and where he can't. Where developers have ignored soil characteristics, grisly tales of seeping septic tanks and streets covered with eroded soil always circulate.

In selecting your homestead, you can make use of soils maps too—if circumstances allow you to take your choice of locations. Find out where the soil conservation office is located in your county seat and go talk to the man in charge there. And listen to what he says. The soil map he will give you for your county (if one is available) will be color coded—sections marked in red, yellow, blue, etc. Each color stands for the particular soil *association* that predominates in that area. An association of soils means just that—the soil is an admixture of two or more kinds of soils, or two or more kinds of soil lie in close proximity to each other. A legend at the bottom of the map gives the names of the soils that each color stands for, plus a brief description of them.

On the other side of the map (at least the ones I'm familiar with) there's a chart which shows the "limitations" of each soil type for selected uses such as farming, homesites, septic tank leach fields, sewage lagoons, lawns, pond construction, pipelines, and highways. If a particular soil is good farming or gardening land, the chart will say "slight limitations for agriculture." For my soil types, the chart says "slight limitations if drained."

25

That means a garden on this soil will do remarkably well if drained with tile and/or surface ditches. Under homesites, a soil might be described as "limited depth to bedrock." That will scare away most developers. "Very slow permeability for leach beds" will make a good developer add plans for sewers past his houses. But such information can be helpful to you, too. On soils of limited permeability, you may have to own a prescribed minimum size acreage for a homesite septic tank. The Environmental Protection Agency is becoming increasingly insistent on this point and is blocking development of much land until proper sewage disposal is provided for. Today, you may build a home with a septic tank, then get hit three years later with a $3,000 sewage assessment you hadn't budgeted for. It happens all the time.

Beyond such considerations, the main aid soil maps can give you is guidance to good places to garden. If gardening is really important to you, or if raising much of your own food is the main reason you want to live in the country, then you will certainly want to narrow your search for a homestead to land the soil surveys say possesses "slight limitations for agriculture." You'll save yourself much time and money in building a good organic soil if you can buy that kind of land. Remember the oldest and best advice ever given to (and by) farmers: "Buy good land if you can; you don't save money buying poor land no matter how cheap it sells for."

Chapter 3

Testing and Evaluating Your Soil

Judging by eye the real or potential productive level of a particular soil is a tricky proposition, even for the most experienced horticulturist or farmer. Telltale signs of fertility or lack of fertility do not always tell the whole tale. Black soils are not always rich nor are stony soils necessarily poor. Ten miles south of my farm lie the Killdeer Plains, whose level black soil used to tempt farmers into buying and farming it. In most cases farming Killdeer land was a journey downhill to failure. Finally people got smart and made a wildlife preserve out of it. At the extreme opposite end of the county are soils so stony a disk will hardly survive on them. But those soils can raise pretty decent crops.

The important part of evaluating a particular soil is not deciding whether it is "rich" or "poor," but rather in assessing accurately *the cost* of producing a good crop on it. Almost any soil can be made productive. A "rich" soil is one that can be improved and maintained in high productivity at much less expense than "poor" soil. In a commercial gardening venture, the expense—the amount of time and money spent—is crucial. If soil "B" demands twice the expense to produce the same amount of vegetables as soil "A", then gardener "B" is only going to make half as much money as gardener "A", or work twice as hard, or both.

It's like buying a used car. You want one that will give you the most miles for the least amount of repair work. You could buy a junker for almost nothing and restore it to a fine running machine, given enough time and money. But how are you going to get to work in the meantime? And an old car is still an old car, even after it's fixed up. The same with poor soil.

Plants tell a lot about the ground they are growing in. Some, like these cattails, grow in swampy areas. Their presence can tell you all you need to know about the gardening potential of this plot: it has almost none.

To determine a soil's fertility, you will (or should) proceed through three successive steps in judgment, the first two before you buy the property, if possible: 1) observe what is growing on top of the ground; 2) study the soil's profile beneath the surface; and 3) have the soil analyzed chemically for nutrient content.

On Top of the Ground

Take a stroll through the neighborhood where you are thinking of buying. If other properties close by display healthy, abundant gardens, you can assume yours will too, even if it's presently overgrown with weeds and brush. If septic tank leach beds are not causing problems in the neighborhood, you can be fairly sure the soil is good for gardening too. Good leach bed action is a sign of deep soil and good permeability. Where leach beds are a problem, a garden will likely need drainage. Level land where water stands in large puddles after rains in summer and where there are numerous ponds in late fall, winter, and early spring, is usually a poor place for a garden or a basement. Creekside soil is almost always rich. But check the area after heavy rains. If the creek floods easily you aren't going to get much of a crop no matter how rich the soil.

In the country, neat, solid farmsteads and prosperous-looking villages almost always reflect rich soil and a vigorous agricultural economy. That is not always true in the Mississippi Delta and other expanses of rich soil where the land owners do not live on the land, or where the farm operators aren't the farm owners.

Plants That Indicate Soil Condition

Certain plants sometimes are a clue to the condition of the soil. Cattails, to use an extreme example, denote wet, marshy soil. Various grasses of the sedge family like nutsedge thrive on rich soil too wet for more desirable grasses. Marsh marigold, joe-pye weed, yellow flag, blue flag, cardinal flower, porcelain vine, loosestrife, skunk cabbage, rose mallow, Japanese iris, pin oak, red maple, swamp white oak, sour gum, weeping willow, black willow, basket willow, Siberian iris, astilbe, bottle gentian, flowering rush, bee balm, boneset, starwort, winterberry, and buttonbush are all plants that like wet soils.

Where burdock, pigweed, lambsquarter, and purslane grow very lush, the soil has good organic content, is fairly well drained and fertile. Fennel, sorrel, mayweed, and chamomile usually mean soil lacking in humus and fertility. Where tiny mosses give the soil surface a greenish tinge that persists into summer, the land is too wet for good gardening and should be tile drained. Broomsedge makes a beautiful golden dye, but where it's growing, the land is generally poor.

Where bluegrass *thrives,* the land is not too acid. The same is even more true of alfalfa. Older farmers would say that any soil that will make a good stand of clover will make a decent living. Walnut trees of good size you'll see almost always on rich ground—usually in a well-drained river or creek bottom soil.

Plants that indicate acid soil include: scrub oak, white cedar, huckleberry, hemlock, fir, blue hydrangea, azalea, trailing arbutus, blueberry, camellia, cranberry, pine, mountain laurel, rhododendron, white birch, and red cedar. Pine and certain other evergreens, as already noted, do not indicate acid soil all the time. They'll grow on neutral soil too. But where these trees grow and reproduce naturally, the ground is usually a little acid.

Under the Soil Surface

The most important evaluation of the soil you can make with your eye is depth of topsoil. The deeper the better of course, but if a plow can turn an eight-inch

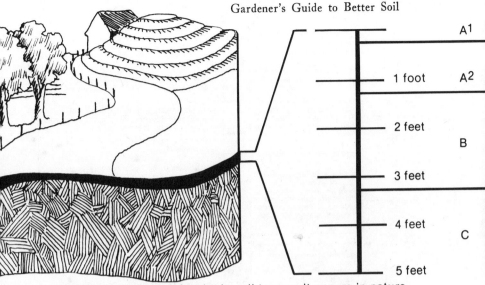

This representation of a single soil type as it occurs in nature reflects the classic major horizons. Just as soil types seldom occur in regular blocks, so too they seldom have all the soil horizons. The chart opposite defines the soil horizons.

furrow without throwing up light-colored subsoil, so much the better.

To get an accurate picture of your soil, you need to see a cross-section of it from the surface to at least five feet down. In soil judging contests, agricultural students dig pits into the earth and smooth the pit sides. The different layers (profiles) of soil are then easy to see distinctly. Sometimes at agricultural fairs, an even larger pit will be dug in the ground with stairs leading down and up. Visitors can get a good look at the composition of the soil that nourishes them.

Much easier than digging a hole is to use a soil auger or a tube probe to take samples of soil from the surface to the five-foot depth or more. The core samples can tell the clay-silt-sand mixture of the various layers. An auger provides a quick way to find out if there's too much gravel in the subsoil to hold water for a pond. A pond that leaks through a gravel and sand bottom is no pond at all.

31

	Organic debris lodged on the soil, usually absent on soils developed from grasses.	Aoo	Loose leaves and organic debris, largely undecomposed.
		Ao	Organic debris partially decomposed or matted.
THE SOLUM (The genetic soil developed by soil-forming processes.)	Horizons of maximum biological activity, of eluviation (removal of materials dissolved or suspended in water), or both.	A1	A dark-colored horizon with a high content of organic matter mixed with mineral matter.
		A2	A light-colored horizon of maximum eluviation. Prominent in Podzolic soils; faintly developed or absent in Chernozemic soils.
		A3	Transitional to B, but more like A than B. Sometimes absent.
	Horizons of illuviation (of accumulation of suspended material from A) or of maximum clay accumulation, or of blocky or prismatic structure, or both.	B1	Transitional to B, but more like B than A. Sometimes absent.
		B2	Maximum accumulation of silicate clay minerals or of iron and organic matter; maximum development of blocky or prismatic structure; or both.
		B3	Transitional to C.
	The weathered parent material. Occasionally absent i.e., soil building may follow weathering such that no weathered material that is not included in the solum is found between B and D.	G	Horizon G for intensely gleyed layers, as in hydromorphic soils.
		Cca / C / Ccs	Horizons Cca and Ccs are layers of accumulated calcium carbonate and calcium sulfate found in some soils.
	Any stratum underneath the soil, such as hard rock or layers of clay or sand, that are not parent material but which may have significance to the overlying soil.	D	

This chart of a classic soil profile has all the principal horizons. Not every horizon will appear in every soil profile.

Sometimes you can find a creek, ditch, or road bank perpendicular enough to reveal soil layers. Then you don't have to dig at all. I make a habit of watching for such banks when visiting farms because a glance will give me a volume of soil history—and I've found Indian arrowheads that way too! Remember when you size up the topsoil depth along a creek bank that you can't assume the same depth in cultivated fields. Erosion may have carried all the topsoil away in the field.

Soil Textures

So let's say you have a smoothed, vertical wall of dirt staring you in the face. It's as good a time as any to become familiar with various soil textures. Take a pinch of soil from each layer in succession. Sand is gritty between your fingers. Silt is powdery, like talcum powder. Clay is hard when dry, greasy when wet, rubbery when moist.

These three substances, sand, silt, and clay, in varying proportions, determine the texture of soil. Sand particles are the largest of the three, measuring from 1/50th of an inch to 1/500th. Silt particles range from 1/500th of an inch to 1/12,500th, and clay particles are less than 1/12,500th of an inch—so small you can't see them with an ordinary microscope. Sand and silt particles are chemically stable in the sense that they remain the same chemical composition as the mother rock from which they came. But not clay particles, which are constantly taking and giving up ions of other elements in the soil. Clay particles form crystals that have a flat, plate-like shape, mostly composed of silica and alumina. The shape seems to make it easy for ions of other elements like nitrates and potassium to become attached so that the clay particles "hold" or "bind" them, as soil scientists would say. That way, nutrients are not washed out of clay soils as easily as they are out of sandy ones. But by the same token, ions of nutrient chemicals "held" by the clay particles might not be freely available for plant food until a different ion is attracted to the clay particle, setting the first one free and thus making it available to plants.

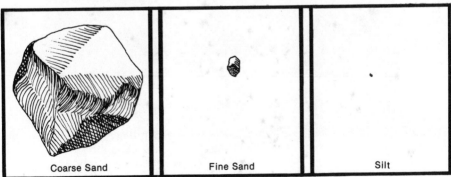

| Coarse Sand | Fine Sand | Silt |

Individual particle sizes vary enormously. At the same magnification as that represented by these drawings, a clay particle remains invisible.

Clay particles and humus are the two storage "tanks" of soil nutrients in which that interaction is constantly taking place. Sand and silt (and to some extent humus) are the texture determiners. A clay soil or what we normally call a clay soil contains about 60 percent clay, 20 percent sand, and 20 percent silt. Clay loam consists of 30 percent sand, 35 percent silt, and 35 percent clay. Loam, the most desirable soil as to texture, contains 40 percent sand, 40 percent silt, and 20 percent clay. Sandy loam is 70 percent sand, 20 percent silt, 10 percent clay; loamy sand, 85 percent sand, 10 percent silt, and 5 percent clay; silt loam, 25 percent sand, 60 percent silt, and 15 percent clay.

An extreme soil condition, one not conducive to a productive garden. When this clay is wet, it is sticky and unworkable. When it is dry, it has a lot of the qualities of masonry. No gardener should be cursed with such soil.

A clayey soil worked when too wet makes a poor seedbed. The soil particles combine in rock-like clods that are difficult to break up and that mass into a rough surface that's tough to penetrate. You can avoid a lot of extra work by holding off the tillage until the soil is sufficiently dried out.

Subsoils

Generally subsoils will be either mostly clay or mostly sand and gravel. Fine-textured (clay) subsoils won't drain well naturally, but coarse-textured sandy or gravelly subsoils cause plants to wither fast in drought conditions.

The presence of rock does not tell you much about soil fertility, but a lot of it close to the surface means hard plowing, disking, and rotary-tilling. Bedrock close to the surface (three feet or closer) most often tells you the soil will be very wet in wet weather and very dry in dry. If you are just selecting a garden site on a

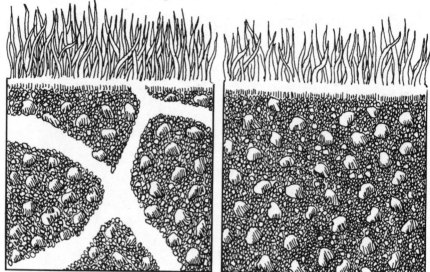

Aeration is depicted here. At left, the soil particles are aggregated to form crumbs. Each crumb is aerated by small pores, and mass of crumbs is aerated by large pores. In sum, the soil is porous and well-aerated. At right, there is no crumb structure, no large pores. The soil is "puddled" and drains poorly.

piece of property where bedrock is close to the surface, probe different spots. Choose the area where bedrock is farthest from the surface for your garden.

If you examine topsoil of land that has been in pasture a long time, you get a good idea of what soil scientists mean by good "crumb" structure. Even in clay soils—in fact, especially in clay soils—land that has been cultivated only by earthworms and grass roots has a loose granular structure that is most desirable. Unfortunately, cultivation tends to destroy the clay "crumbs" or to break them up into individual particles that pack tight and hard.

By using great care, you can sometimes clear the soil away from roots along the face of your soil profile to examine how far the latter have been able to penetrate into the subsoil. The further the better. Short, fat taproots of weeds mean hard soil in which root vegetables like carrots are not going to attain much size.

Where roots of grasses and legumes reach a level about eight to ten inches down and then seem to be blocked or turned sideways, a hardpan may have formed. Constant plowing at the same depth over a number of years causes a compaction of the soil at plow depth that stops root growth and both moisture and air transpiration between soil surface and subsoil. That's hardpan. Unless your garden was formerly a part of a farm field, a hardpan is not something you have to worry about.

Gray flecks dotted through clay subsoil are probably limestone and that's good. Reddish soils (or rocks) usually denote iron. Black can mean good humus content, but may mean nothing more than manganese-bearing rock particles. Tans, light grays, light bluish grays in clay regularly reveal poor soil, but subsoils of these colors often contain good supplies of minerals.

If the hole you dug to study the soil fills up with water, wait awhile before you buy a tiller. You may want a rowboat instead.

Testing Your Soil

There are many do-it-yourself soil testing kits on the market, any of which can provide hours of rainy day or winter fun. I can't think of a better Christmas gift for a gardener. You'll even learn a few facts about chemicals that you should have learned in high school instead of worrying about whom you were taking to the prom.

Even I managed to discover that my soil had enough nitrogen in it (which I suspected from looking at the plants) and that the soil pH was about 6 (what I surmised it was). I found that my soil seemed to need phosphorus and potash, too.

So why am I not sold on do-it-yourself soil testing? First of all, if you're not trained in chemistry, you're never sure of what you're doing. Secondly, if you're

37

short on potash, for instance, the next question is: compared to what? Soil laboratories see the results of hundreds of tests of similar soils in a region and use this frame of reference to interpret their analyses when recommending what and how much fertilizer a specific soil situation needs. An individual gardener can't do that.

Interpreting the results of soil testing is the heart of the matter, not the soil test itself, and the best laboratory (to say nothing of little old me and my handy-dandy soil testing kit) can make a mistake. For instance: a soil sample comes into a good laboratory which analyzes it

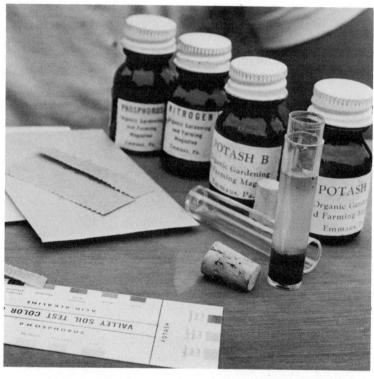

An elaborate and expensive soil test kit isn't necessary. A simple kit such as this is sufficient to check your garden soil for major nutrient deficiencies and soil reaction (pH).

not only for major nutrients (N-P-K) but for micronutrients (trace elements) as well. The sample, according to the tests, has enough trace element manganese in it, so the lab does not recommend adding that element to the fertilizer. However, the soil sample came from ground where a patch of beans sported sickly yellow leaves. The ground was a tight clay where water would stay in wet weather, but the trouble was not wetness because very little rain had fallen since the sickly beans had been planted. Soil sleuths, visiting the spot, are able to determine the answer to the riddle. There is sufficient manganese in the soil along with enough major elements, but the manganese was not *available* to the plant.

That's getting down to the fine points of soil management, and I might add that the experts did not agree on what to do about that particular situation. But the lesson is that *what's right in the laboratory is not always what's right in the field*.

The First Step

Nevertheless, laboratory testing is the first step any serious gardener should take if he's faced with improving a poor soil or stumped by a problem he can't overcome in an otherwise good soil. Agricultural colleges in almost every state have soil testing services at very low cost to people within their respective states. The service is usually conducted under the auspices of the Extension Service, and you should contact your own local County Extension Agent who will tell you how, when, and where to send in your samples. Reputable private laboratories also test soil. They charge more but will often do more. Some send their own personnel to the field to take the samples. The labs will run any test you are willing to pay for, including analysis for organic matter content, pesticide content, or for any of the trace elements. I don't know of any dishonest labora-

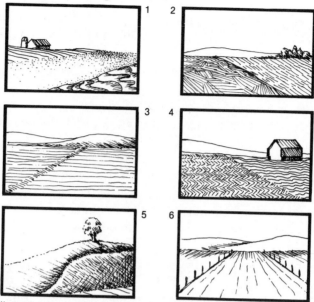

Soils and soil conditions vary greatly, so it is imperative to study the garden site carefully so a representative soil sample is tested. A farmer does this, and so should a gardener. The farm in sketch one has a field with three different soils, a clay, a sandy loam and a muck. A sample from each soil should be tested. Sketch two represents a field that was partially limed several years ago. Sketch three depicts two fields that have been joined. Sketch four depicts a field that was heavily manured on one half last year and not at all on the other half. Due to the management differences in these fields, two separate samples from each of the three should be tested. Sketch five shows a well-drained gentle slope, a well-drained steep slope and a poorly drained flat area. The topographical and drainage variations dictate three separate test samples. In the case of the sixth sketch, the field, though uniform in soil and condition, is so large that three separate samples should be tested.

tories, but common sense should dictate to you that any lab that is closely allied to a particular fertilizer company may be inclined to make soil analyses which show the best solution to your problem is that particular fertilizer.

Sampling Techniques

To take soil samples from your land properly, first do a little thinking and reconnoitering. Determine how many different soil tests you are going to need. You may need only one, if your whole garden is the same kind of soil on the same kind of slope, hilltop, or valley. In that case you need to take about six samplings from different places more or less equally spaced apart and mix them together for one sample.

If your property contains decidedly different types of soil, take two or three samplings from each site to mix together, but keep the different site samples separated. For instance, if you have a big hill in back of your property where you have lawn or a small pasture and you have a garden on low ground at the other end of your property, you will want two different tests made. When you send in the two samples, specify that you want recommendations for growing lawn or pasture on the

At the New Organic Gardening Experimental Farm in Maxatawny, Pennsylvania, soil testing, beginning with carefully acquired representative soil samples, is a part of every garden experiment. Here a core sample is taken in a section of the garden before the season's second vegetable crop is planted.

one, and recommendations for growing vegetables on the other.

On larger acreages, sampling is almost always done by field, because any treatment a farmer uses, he will apply to the whole field, generally speaking. On a ten-acre field you might take six samplings from various spots and mix them together for one sample, marked "Field A" or whatever. And so on, for each field.

What you want is a *representative* sample. In the lab, the actual testing will be done with about a teaspoon of soil, and you want that small amount to accurately reflect conditions on an acre or maybe twenty acres of your soil.

The best time to take your samplings is in the fall, on a day the soil is fairly dry. Spring is OK too, but that season is the busy time for labs, and you may get recommendations back too late to act upon them.

A sampling probe (left) is the best tool to use for getting soil samples for testing. But a specialized tool isn't necessary. Just use a garden trowel, excavating a small hole, then shaving a half-inch slice of soil from the surface to a depth of six to eight inches. This slice should be mixed thoroughly with samples from several other spots within the area of soil to be tested. This technique will put far more soil into the sample than is needed for testing, but it will best provide a sample representative of the soil in the garden.

Use a trowel or spade to take a sampling of soil. Dig in about six inches, so the sampling contains dirt from the surface down to that depth. Don't just skim dirt off the top of the ground. A trowel full of dirt is plenty, per sampling. Mix the samplings from one site together well in a bucket, and keep enough to fill a small paper bag half-full. If the soil is wet, you will have to dry it out before mixing. Use a clean plastic bucket if at all possible so that no foreign element—like rust or metal from a tin bucket—gets into the soil and influences the analysis.

Evaluating the Results

Results of the tests and the university's (or private lab's) recommendations will be sent to you about six weeks after you send in the samples. Maybe sooner.

If you've chosen to get a thorough analysis of your garden's soil, you'll get figures on the presence (or absence) of the major nutrients—nitrogen, phosphorus, and potassium—and the micronutrients (trace elements). You'll get a reading on whether your soil is acid or alkaline and an indication of the level of humus in your soil. Subsequent chapters will relate what these things mean in your garden.

But in general, the test results—even the relatively unspecific results of tests you might conduct—will give you a direction for soil building efforts. Tests done by a state agricultural school or a private testing laboratory will usually come with recommendations for fertilization. In having any soil test done, specify that you'd like recommendations for organic materials; you might get them, but probably not. What you'll probably get is something like the following: "Use 200 pounds of limestone per 1,000 square feet. Use ten pounds of 10-10-10 per 1,000 square feet at planting. Side dress with three pounds of ammonium nitrate per 1,000 square feet during the growing season." And the question you'll ask yourself (if no one else) is: what does that mean in organic terms?

Here's how the editors of *Organic Gardening and Farming* suggest interpreting such test recommendations: Suppose your garden is 40 by 60 feet. That's 2,400 square feet, or about a sixteenth of an acre. First, follow the limestone application recommendation of 200 pounds per 1,000 square feet by putting down about 500 pounds of crushed limestone. Next, forget about trying to find an organic fertilizer with an analysis of 10-10-10. For nitrogen, use manure. The optimum rate for manuring cropland is about fifteen tons per acre. Thus, you'll need about a ton for your sixteenth of an acre garden. The phosphorus and potassium the recom-

TABLE 1
FERTILIZATION SCHEDULE
Larry and Betsy Robins' Garden

	Plot 1 (25x50 feet)	Plot 2 (25x50 feet)	Plot 3 (50x100 feet)
1970	–	–	1000 lbs. crushed limestone 400 lbs. rock phosphate 400 lbs. granite dust Manure (10 tons/acre) Cover crop planted in fall.
1971	–	–	200 lbs. granite dust 200 lbs. rock phosphate Manure (10 tons/acre) Cover crop planted in fall.
1972	–	100 lbs. limestone, rock phosphate and granite dust. Manured. Cover crop planted in fall.	200 lbs. rock phosphate 200 lbs. granite dust Manure (10 tons/acre) (No cover crop this year)
1973	100 lbs. limestone, rock phosphate, granite dust. Manured. Cover crop planted in fall.	Same as previous year only no limestone.	200 lbs. rock phosphate 200 lbs. granite dust Manure (10 tons/acre) Cover crop planted in fall.

NOTE: In addition, all plots received four inches of thick spoiled hay mulch each year. Compost is added to the planting rows themselves before turning them under in the fall and is used as a planting medium in the rows in the spring.

mendations call for—along with some trace minerals—will undoubtedly be provided by the manure. If you want more, apply 100 pounds each of rock phosphate and greensand or granite powder annually for three years, for up to seven or eight years of fertilizing action.

The tested results of one such organic soil building program were reported in the December 1973 issue of *OGF*. Larry and Betsy Robins started gardening one plot at their Pennsylvania home, then started a second and a third plot. The charts reveal the way the plots were fertilized, and the results of very complete soil tests (with the control reflecting the status of the soil they started with). I'll let you draw you own conclusions.

TABLE 2

SOIL TEST ON LARRY ROBINS' GARDEN

Fredericksville, Pa.

Analysis	Control (No treatment)	Plot 1 1 year treatment	Plot 2 2 years treatment	Plot 3 3 years treatment	Satisfactory Levels of Nutrients
pH	6.1	6.2	6.7	7.4	6.0-7.5
Humus, %	3.84	4.33	6.60	7.62	Above 3%
Nitrogen	1350	1686	2323	2405	500-3000
Phosphorus	7	9	13	48	20-60
Potassium	67	86	148	160	100-150
Calcium	900	1016	1855	2476	750-1500
Magnesium	37	102	154	179	150-250
Sodium	131	84	154	171	1-1000
Sulfur	23	29	37	42	10-1000
Boron	0.84	0.54	0.60	0.74	0.5-1.0
Iron	1.56	1.57	1.34	1.72	1.0-8.0
Manganese	2.46	1.79	3.16	4.19	2.0-8.0
Zinc	0.89	0.84	1.54	1.73	1.0-2.0

COMMENTS: All values except humus (percent) and pH are given in ppm. The availability of B, Fe, Mn, and Zn increases below pH 6.5. Higher values may be indicated at lower pH.

Chapter 4

The Three
Major Plant Foods

When the results of your soil tests are mailed back to you, the main message they'll bring (besides your soil pH) is the nitrogen (N), phosphorus (P), and potash (K) content of your soil. These three elements are called the major nutrients and are so important to plant life that without adequate amounts of them you can kiss your gardening efforts goodbye.

Supplying nitrogen, phosphorus, and potash at rates recommended by soil tests has become an extremely sophisticated process when chemicals are used. Because chemicals can be applied at *exact* rates, recommendations may call for a certain number of pounds per acre of, say, a 20-36-18 fertilizer broadcast ahead of planting followed by so many pounds per acre of a 6-14-8 directly beside the seed in the row. The numbers refer to the percent of NPK in the fertilizer mix. With bulk blending of fertilizers, farmers can order any oddball mixture they wish and many of them do just that. I think there is a certain amount of posturing to the practice—there's status in tossing around esoteric fertilizer mixtures in your conversations with other farmers, and chemical salesmen know it.

As noted in the last chapter, organic gardeners can't play that game as well, because organic fertilizers aren't usually a standardized commodity always containing the same amounts of NPK. Moreover, the organic gardener has no reason to get so precious over fertilizer rates. He believes if he maintains a balanced fertility in his soil, the plants growing there will do just fine. His yields won't always be as high as if he'd employed all that modern science knows about chemical fertilizers, but they'll be adequate and of better quality.

Nitrogen

Soils rich in organic matter are seldom deficient in nitrogen, since nitrogen is produced during decomposition of organic matter. The amount may not be high enough to produce top yields, however. That's why soil periodically should be planted to a legume that will fix additional nitrogen in the soil by the action of bacteria living on the legume roots. Since there are about 75 million pounds of nitrogen in the air above every acre of land, the amount of nitrogen fixed by legumes is limited only by the plant's ability to do the fixing. Some day—and researchers are working at it already—we may have legumes and bacteria which will supply all the nitrogen a soil needs without any help from additional fertilizer.[2] But for now there will be times when a soil needs additional help in building up a sufficient supply of nitrogen. This is particularly true for gardeners who take over poor ground and want to raise good crops immediately. It takes nature years to restore a soil's fertility. With organic help, the natural process can be speeded up.

47

Growing and consuming plants, in some other way than allowing them to rot back into the soil from which they sprang, are activities which are by their nature nitrogen depleting. If you don't put back as much as you take out of the soil, you're losing ground—literally. The process to me is sort of like money and banks. If you establish a savings account and draw no money out of it, the interest keeps accumulating. Your money increases without any particular effort on your part. If, on the other hand, you don't have a savings account but must borrow money steadily, then you must always be paying back—principal plus interest. If you have more nitrogen "banked" in the soil in the form of organic matter than you are taking out, the soil continues to build up—progressively, like interest on savings. You don't just hang on by the skin of your teeth each year in your gardening. And if a year comes when you can't get extra fertilizer from outside sources, there's enough in your "bank" to tide you over. But if you haven't practiced thrift—if you've taken out more nitrogen than you've left in—you have to pay back from another source with interest. And you can't ride out a bad year of fertilizer shortages.

Balancing the Supply

Plants can't use nitrogen in its raw form. First acids in the soil change it to nitrate forms which the roots then take up. In the plant cells the nitrate salts are converted to amino acids of many kinds which recombine to form protein. And protein, of course, is the real staff of life.

You can upset the process by which nitrogen becomes protein either by not providing enough of the former or by providing too much. Too little in a vegetable garden makes plants spindly and yellowish; too much and they grow rank, producing too much stem and leaf in relation to fruit, or producing leaf which has small protein value.

Too much nitrogen can make grains, especially wheat, grow so rank that they fall over at the first heavy rain or hard wind. In very dry weather, an excess of nitrogen fertilizer can build nitrate levels in stunted plants high enough to cause nitrate poisoning.

Nitrogen Deficiency

You can spot nitrogen deficiency in your garden sometimes by color. Vegetable plants well supplied with nitrogen are a rich, dark green and grow fast in warm, humid weather. When growth is slow and plant color yellowish-green, you're most likely short on nitrogen. First the leaves yellow, then the stems. In case of nitrogen starvation, the whole plant turns yellow, then brown. Kaput. A tomato plant lacking nitrogen grows very slowly. The younger leaves on the top of the plant fail to reach full size, then begin to yellow. Flower buds shed. Fruits that develop are small and hard, light green when unripe, but turn a very vivid red when ripe.

Yellowing of leaves occurs from other causes, so be forewarned. Even experts cannot always tell by sight alone. On ground not properly drained, the yellowing may mean that nitrogen is not available to the plant because of excessive moisture and lack of aeration, even though enough of the nutrient is actually present in the soil.

Nitrogen Surplus

You can often observe how grass, especially blue-grass, will grow lush and heavy around manure droppings in a pasture field. Cows will seldom eat this grass though it looks to be the most delicious in the field. The grass has taken up excessive amounts of nitrates from the manure, creating the possibility of nitrate poisoning. The cow doesn't know that, but she knows she doesn't like the taste of that grass. Organicists who have observed that bug damage to healthy, vigorous plants is less than to weaker plants are probably witnessing the same situation. Plants abundantly supplied with nitrogen may taste as bad to leaf-eating bugs as grass oversupplied with nitrates tastes to cattle.

If nitrogen can build-in a certain amount of bug resistance to a plant, it has the opposite effect in regard to fungal diseases. Plants abundantly supplied are more susceptible. You win some, lose some.

Long-lasting, slow-release organic nitrogen is such a good fertilizer it goes on working in the fall when you'd just as soon it didn't. In some cases, bush fruits, like raspberries, will grow vigorously in the fall on rich ground (especially if the fall is wet) and that growth may winterkill. Try to apply high nitrogen fertilizers to such plants only in spring or early summer.

Nitrogen Sources

Which nitrogen fertilizer is better, organic or inorganic chemical?[3] I don't think there's a soil scientist who will not admit that organic methods are a better way to handle the soil than with bags of chemicals.

As to which kind of soil—organically handled or chemically treated—produces the tastier fruits and vegetables, there's no disputing tastes. I know two brothers who prefer canned peas to fresh ones. But I find it hard to see how certain chemical champions dismiss the possibility that soil management can influence the taste of the crop.[4] Too much nitrogen, especially if accompanied by too little potassium and lots of water, produces less tasty vegetables, especially corn and melons. This is particularly true if the nitrogen comes from a bag of chemicals and the water is irrigation water, not rain. Experienced gardeners know that. So if some cultural practices change the taste of the product, why not admit the possibility that other practices might change taste too?

Manures

Animal manures remain the best all-around organic fertilizer. They are not as high in nitrogen as some other organic sources, but they are still available in quantity in many areas and they build organic matter content at a faster rate than most other organic fertilizers. Manures vary in nitrogen content: rabbit droppings contain 2½ percent on the average, and poultry manure 1½ percent. Hog and cow manure have the lowest content of nitrogen of all barnyard manures. That's why they are rarely used in hotbeds—not enough nitrogen to make the heap under the hotbed get hot. Horse manure is the preferred hotbed manure.[5]

(*Handling*) The fertility value of manure depends also on the way it's handled. If piled out in the weather unprotected, the manure loses nutrients that leach away in falling rain. Pound for pound, rotted manure kept

A rich mixture of manure and bedding remains the best fertilizer there is. Each forkful contains all the major nutrients, many if not all of the micro-nutrients, and organic matter. Manure has always been central to the organic method.

POULTRY MANURE (Without Litter)

Nitrogen (%N)	Phosphorus (%P)	Potassium (%K)	Calcium (%CaCO$_3$)	Magnesium (%MgCO$_3$)	Boron (p.p.m.B)
2.00	1.88	1.85	2.5	0.4	5

FRESH TURKEY MANURE

Nitrogen (%N)	Phosphorus (%P)	Potassium (%K)
1.31	0.31	0.41

BROILER (Poultry) MANURE

Nitrogen (%N)	Phosphorus (%P)	Potassium (%K)
2.30	1.08	1.69

RABBIT MANURE

Nitrogen (%N)	Phosphorus (%P)	Potassium (%K)
2.40	0.62	0.05

indoors is richer than fresh because it contains less water and is more compact. The nitrogen in rotted manure is not as available as in fresh manure, which is why fresh manure "burns" plants sometimes when it is applied too close to them.

The value of manure is usually increased by the amount of bedding mixed into it because the bedding absorbs the animal urine. Urine is richer in nitrogen and potash than are solid wastes. The straw itself, in addition to the organic matter it supplies, contains a trace of phosphorus plus about a half percent each of nitrogen and potash.

(*Application*) In applying manure to the soil, farmers and gardeners have always been exhorted to plow, disk, or rotary till the manure into the soil immediately after it is spread. It's an arguable point. If you spread manure on frozen ground, rain or a quick thaw may wash the nutrients into the river rather than into the soil. But manure spread on the land in August will, in the event of rain, leach most of its nutrients right into the top layer of the soil where they belong. There they work more beneficially than if buried six to eight inches deep by plowing. That's why a thin layer of manure spread on pastures, lawns, or growing hay crops does so much good.

MAJOR NUTRIENTS IN COW MANURE (WITH BEDDING)

Nutrients In Pounds Per Ton

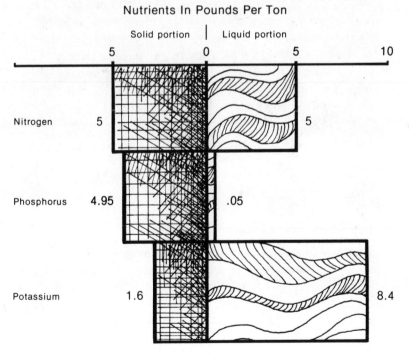

The very best way to use manures in the garden is
to compost them, then use the resultant material as a
fertilizer, dribbling it into the planting trench with the
seed. Composting is a high labor project that can be
made easier two ways. The first is with chickens. Simply
bed them with straw, old hay, or any organic material
and let the bedding build up for a year. The chickens,
by scratching for grain and other food bits, compost
the bedding and manure into a very good, high-nitrogen-
ous fertilizer. The second way is sheet composting—
spreading manure as mulch six or more inches deep
around garden plants and between rows. Nature will
compost it slowly into humus. In the meantime, the
mulch suppresses weeds and preserves moisture.

A normally adequate application of manure is a ten
tons-per-acre rate. Fifteen tons is better if you can get
it and have the time to apply it. Over twenty tons and
you may run into the danger of too much nitrogen. But
because nitrogen content of manure can vary so much,
these rates of application are merely approximations—
kind of whistling in the dark. In the garden twenty-five
pounds of manure of the dried kind you buy in bags will
take care of 100 square feet of garden, if you apply it
alongside the rows only. For mulching with stable ma-

PERCENTAGES OF FERTILIZING CONSTITUENTS IN URINE OF VARIOUS FARM ANIMALS AND VALUE IN RELATION TO TOTAL EXCREMENTS

Animal	Nitrogen %	Phosphoric oxide %	Potash %	Value %
Horse	35	0	58	50
Cattle	53	5	71	65
Sheep	63	4	86	75
Hogs	32	13	55	40

PROPORTION OF FERTILIZING CONSTITUENTS AND ORGANIC MATTER OF FARM MANURES, INCLUDING LITTER, THAT IS SOLUBLE IN WATER

Animal	Organic Matter %	Nitrogen %	Phosphoric oxide %	Potash %
Horse	5	53	53	76
Dairy cow	7	50	50	97
Steer	7	56	36	92
Sheep	7	42	58	97

nure, use at least a forkful for every square foot.

(*Manure Production*) There's a formula for determining the amount of manure each kind of barnyard animal produces a year. You weigh how much the animal is fed and then for a horse multiply by 2.1, for a cow 3.8, for a sheep 1.8, and for a chicken 1.6. Add to that the amount of bedding used. This formula won't work for grazing animals, but then you don't collect the droppings from grazing animals either. Another way to figure your fertilizer profits in manure, you homesteaders, is to use the rule of thumb that says a horse will produce about nine tons of manure a year and a cow about eleven tons. Figure three tons for a 200-pound hog, a half ton for a market-sized lamb, and seven tons a year for 100 laying hens. Then calculate the value of the manure as a replacement for fertilizers you would otherwise have to buy. That seven tons of poultry manure, for instance, should contain about 280 pounds of nitrogen, 250 pounds of phosphoric acid, and 140 pounds of potash. If you put that manure on an acre of ground and planted it to corn, you should get a yield of around 125 to 150 bushels per acre, everything else being equal. And that's about how much grain you'll need from an acre to keep 100 hens year-round. Right now, the cost of the commercial fertilizer you'd need to raise that much corn on an acre, if you didn't have the hen manure, would be in excess of $180. The commercial fertilizer would not give you the organic matter or trace elements the hen manure does.

Cottonseed Meal

Cottonseed meal is perhaps the second best source of organic nitrogen. It contains around 7 percent nitrogen, which is good for an organic product. Somewhat acid, cottonseed meal is an ideal nitrogen fertilizer around acid-loving plants like azalea and blueberry. On garden vegetables, it is best to apply lime along with cottonseed meal if you use the latter regularly. The meal is not always available since so much of it goes to the cattle feeding market. There it's sold as a high protein supplement, cottonseed cake.

Feather Meal

Feather meal, containing about 12 percent nitrogen, makes excellent use of one of the by-products of the broiler business. The feathers are cooked, then dried and ground into meal. If you want a truly slow-release fertilizer, feather meal is the one to choose. It is excellent for applying with your green manure crop.

Bloodmeal

Bloodmeal is one of the richest sources of organic nitrogen you can buy, but the trouble is that you can't buy much of it. Bloodmeal is collected in slaughter-houses, dried and ground. It's too scarce and expensive to use in quantity—a twenty-five pound bag was selling for about fifteen dollars in mid-1974. But the small gardener, needing a lot of nitrogen in a hurry, can get good results with this 12 percent nitrogen fertilizer. Tankage, scraps of waste meat and fat, is a similar source of nitrogen. The animal feed industry uses large amounts of tankage and dried blood as protein supplements in its feed mixes.

Fish

Fish scraps are high in nitrogen too. I've often thought there were four ideal places for an organic farmer to live: near a feedlot-packing house operation where lots of manure and meat wastes would be available; near a mushroom farm where he could get good supplies of spent mushroom compost; near a vegetable cannery where scads of vegetable waste could be had for the hauling; or near a commercial fishing port where fish scraps and seaweed could be found in quantity.

Sewage Sludge

Activated sludge can analyze as high as 5 percent nitrogen. It's called "activated" to distinguish it from "digested" sludge. Activated means that air is forced through the sewage causing bubbling which speeds up bacterial action. The bacteria coagulate the organic matter which then settles out of the water, leaving a clear liquid that can be discharged into streams with less danger of pollution. In "digested" sludge, the organic matter settles out by gravity and the water is drained off. Both sludges are good soil conditioners, but the activated type contains more nitrogen and hence makes a better fertilizer for lawns, shrubs, and trees.

Activated sludge is generally heat-treated for sterilization purposes before being made into fertilizer. Such fertilizers are now gaining wide acceptance and are in demand from golf course caretakers especially. No doubt as other sources of nitrogen become scarce and more expensive and as city waste disposal becomes more sophisticated, sludge fertilizers will come into their own and solve both the fertilizer problem on the farm and the waste problem in the cities.

When applying sludge to ground where a lawn is to be started, mix it thoroughly with the soil. Follow recommendations on the bag—application should be between twenty-five and fifty pounds per 100 square feet—or fifteen tons per acre.

Is sludge safe on food crops? It's not yet recommended on vegetables or other plants parts of which are eaten directly, but otherwise most of the experts consider it quite safe as a soil amendment (see note 21). Some people are afraid that a plant fertilized with sludge will take some kind of foul matter up into its fibers which could be transferred to fruit even—if the plant were a tree—and from there to the eater of the fruit. I have a personal experience that will set your mind at ease on this score. The elderberries we often gather and eat grow along the edge of an open sewage ditch along a railroad track. There really is foul matter in that ditch. That's where the roots of the elderberry plants get their nourishment to produce the biggest, juiciest elderberries ever. People have been eating these berries for years and the ones I know are disgustingly healthy.

Phosphorus

Gardeners are very much aware of the close relationship between organic matter and nitrogen, but the decomposition of organic matter in the soil is of equal importance to the amount of phosphorus available to plants. In both sandy and clay soils, phosphates can become quickly unavailable—"locked up"—in the absence of rotting organic matter. The carbonic and nitric acids present as organic matter break down and help unlock the phosphorus.

Without phosphorus, plant growth slows. Crops won't mature when they should. Scientists are not positive yet about what phosphorus does, but they think the following explanation is accurate. The cellular material that mysteriously pulls the cell interior apart to form two new cells contains phosphorus. If the content is low, the rate of cell division is slow.

The subject of phosphorus deficiency gives me an excuse to inveigh against a press release issued by our land grant colleges periodically. The purpose of the release seems to be to hit organic gardening a good lick just on general principles, gain attention, and prove to the old alma mater that here is one researcher who has not wavered from the path of chemical righteousness. An expert is invariably quoted to the effect that "Food grown on poor soil is no less nutritious than food grown on good soil. The variation is only one of quantity."

How can responsible people utter statements like that? Outside a very, very, narrow context, that is plain, unvarnished error. Phosphorus deficiency is one of many examples that will refute such a declaration. Cows pastured on soil lacking phosphorus have poor bone development. Such a cow can look like the living death walking around. Check the University of Minnesota and ask to see their photos of cows grazed on poor, phosphorus-deficient soils in northern Minnesota. If we humans didn't get adequate phosphorus in our diets, we'd start looking like those knock-kneed, mangy cows. Right before we died.[6]

Phosphorus Deficiency

The quickest, surest indicator of phosphorus deficiency in vegetable plants is a reddish-purple discolora-

A prime source of phosphorus for the organic garden is colloidal clay residues of phosphate mining in Florida. Originally considered waste, the residues are now being dug up and processed. The resultant product is 18 percent phosphoric acid and 15 percent calcium, and has an abundance of trace minerals as well.

tion of leaves, leaf veins, and stems. The coloring comes from an over-concentration of sugar resulting in the formation of anthocyanin, a purple pigment—the same reddish purple you see in autumn leaves. The excessive sugar production is triggered by the scanty supply of phosphorus.

Corn leaves, including sweet corn, may first appear a darker green than usual when young if phosphorus is lacking. Then the leaves and stalks become purplish. Knee-high corn with purple-fringed leaves almost always reveals that your land needs phosphorus. Defectively shaped ears are another sign—the crooked ears caused by slow silk emergence at pollination time. Crooked and incomplete rows of kernels on the ear is another sign.

Tomatoes starved for phosphorus get the characteristic reddish-purple color on the underside of their leaves, the color first appearing in spots on the web of the leaf, spreading to the entire leaf, and finally affecting the veins. Leaves are small and stalks too slender.

Cole vegetables turn reddish purple too, on leaf edges. But don't confuse that with purple cabbage! Also some sweet corn, like Early Sunrise, has a purplish hue in the stalks, natural to the variety. Remember, too, that cane sorghum shows reddish blotches on the stalk because of high sugar content, but it's *supposed* to have high sugar content.

Supplying Phosphorus

A good, built-up organic soil seldom if ever shows phosphorus deficiency because where high organic matter content is maintained, the natural phosphorus in the soil remains more available. But every soil, no matter how good, should have phosphorus added to it periodically if the soil is heavily cropped. Phosphate rock, either raw or the colloidal type, is the accepted organic fertilizer to apply. Rock phosphate is not cheap, but a two ton per acre application once every four years won't break you up either. An eighty pound bag costs in the neighborhood of $2.50 (mid-1974) and bulk by the ton runs around $55.

Rock phosphate is not as readily soluble in water as superphosphate, though modern crushers can now render the former to a very fine powder that allows the phosphorus to be released much faster than used to be the case. Moreover, in the presence of lots of organic matter, more phosphoric acid becomes available from slow release sources like phosphate rock than the superphosphate salesmen will admit.[7] Organicists don't use superphosphate for a number of reasons. They figure the extra processing necessary to convert rock phosphate into superphosphate represents a use of energy unnecessary to organic agriculture. The sulfuric acid used to make the conversion causes a build-up of a type of bacteria in the soil which feed on fungi that break down cellulose, organicists also maintain. The oversupply of sulfur causes oversupply of the bacteria and a resultant undersupply of cellulose-eating fungi so necessary in the decomposition of organic matter. Moreover, it seems that the sulfuric acid makes the boron and zinc in the rock phosphate unavailable.

You should apply about ten pounds of rock phosphate per 100 square feet of garden space *along with* twenty-five pounds of manure.[8] Put the manure on first, work the ground, then add the rock phosphate a month or two later. Sprinkle the ground phosphate on the soil just as you would lime and, if possible, work it into the top inch of soil. Or just let the rain work it in. Spread on lawns the same way, one pound per ten square feet.

Bone meal is another source of phosphorus that makes sense a small garden or on a few choice shrubs around the house. There are three kinds of bone fertilizer products: raw bone meal, steamed bone meal, and bone black, all with a phosphorus content of over 20 percent, though exact content will vary according to the age, diet, and kind of animal the bones come from.

Some disagreement exists among gardeners over the benefits of bone meal. Some say they get no results from it; others wouldn't garden without it. The difference of opinion probably springs from the fact that it takes a long time for the meal to decompose and release the phosphorus in it. Also, gardeners who really care enough to use bone meal usually already have soil in good shape. A fifty-pound bag of bone meal runs about $7 and a five-pound bag $1.50 (1974 prices). Raw bone meal also has a relatively high nitrogen content and because of the calcium and lime in it will help reduce soil acidity.

Potassium

The third major plant food is potassium, more commonly referred to as potash when talking about fertilizer. Potassium is certainly the most elusive plant food. In one acre of ground there may be 40,000 pounds of potassium in the top six inches of soil, but only 1 percent of it might be immediately available. Potassium seems to be needed for all the functions of the plant, but the plant does not build it into the structure of its parts. The element may move back into the soil as the plant matures. It also moves around in the plant, usually going from older to younger tissue. Once the plant dies, the potassium is very easily leached out of it.

Scientists don't know yet exactly why potassium is so important to plants. It just is. The most commonly held theory is that potassium helps the plant resist disease, protects it from cold, and protects it during dry weather by preventing excessive losses of water. It also helps in the formation of plant sugars.

Potassium Deficiency

A plant lacking potassium grows slower. The leaves may get yellow streaks in them. Edges and tips of leaves become dry and scorched. In corn, the ears that do develop are often just nubbins and on the stalks, the space between leaf nodes is abnormally foreshortened. The dwarfing makes the whole stalk shorter and the leaves appear too long for the plant. Stalks of corn or other grains are generally weak where potassium is in short supply and will break or blow over more easily.

In tomatoes, potassium shortage stunts plants. The young leaves become wrinkled, older leaves grayish and yellow along the edges. Light-colored spots between veins turn eventually to a bright orange color before the leaves die. Fruits, if any, ripen unevenly and are abnormally soft. Cabbage along leaf borders turns bronze-colored, then a scorched brown. In carrots, the leaves curl. Beets grow tapered roots instead of fat bulbs. Radishes first show unusually deep green in the center of the leaf and scorching on the edges later.

Supplying Potassium

Potash is the most difficult fertilizer for organic growers to obtain in quantity, and therefore presents the biggest problem in any large-scale organic venture. Muriate of potash is the main source of potash fertilizer in the United States, but is not recommended nor certified by organic gardeners even though it is mined from natural deposits laid down by ancient oceans. The potash in these deposits is potassium chloride salts, and organicists claim that both the salts and the chlorine in them leave residues that are harmful to the soil.

Instead, organic growers use greensand, also an oceanic deposit. Sometimes called glauconite or glauconite potash, greensand contains approximately 7 percent potash—all in a form available to plants. Greensand is actually more of a granulated clay than a sand, which helps explain why it absorbs and holds water to further aid plant growth. Greensand also contains silica, iron, lime, and phosphorus, plus traces of many other elements. Traditional recommendations call for an application rate of ¼ pound per square foot. That's fine for small gardens, but you may want to spread it thinner on larger plots or fields. Greensand sells for about three dollars for a sixty-pound bag.

Granite dust is more often used as potash fertilizer by organic farmers. It contains from 3 percent to 5½ percent potash. Some experimenters have gotten remarkable performance from granite dust, considering its relatively low potash content compared to muriate of potash. Years ago, the University of Connecticut, looking for a potash fertilizer for that state's specialized tobacco industry, tried a high-grade granite dust in place of the usual nitrate of potash, sulfate of potash, or potassium carbonate—all of which have some disadvantages for tobacco. Used at a rate of two tons to the acre along with regular chemical nitrogen and phosphorus, the granite stone gave as good a performance on yield and quality of the tobacco as other more potent forms of potash. Granite dust, however, has not caught on outside the organic field since muriate of potash has been cheaper—at least by the bulk volume. But if other fossil sources of potash begin to run out, granite dust will get wider attention again. Best application is ten pounds to 100 square feet every three years or whenever you turn over a cover crop.

The richest organic source of potash is wood ashes, especially hardwood ashes as mentioned earlier. Seaweed, tobacco stems, fish scraps, and cottonseed meal contain worthwhile amounts of potash too. Green alfalfa hay can contain about 2 percent potash, no doubt pulled up from deep in the subsoil by the long alfalfa roots. When the alfalfa plants die, the potash will easily leach away, but if the plants are worked into the soil as green manure, the potash is saved.[9]

Chapter 5

Micronutrients:
A Little Dab Will Do It

In addition to the major nutrients, there must be present in the soil, in available form, small but critical amounts of zinc, manganese, boron, iron, sulfur, copper, magnesium, molybdenum, and chlorine—at least. Other elements may be necessary though their functions are not yet well understood. Among these are such far-out elements as barium, vanadium, strontium, silver, and titanium. Still other elements, while not necessary for the plants as far as is known, are absolutely essential to the health of animals eating the plants. Selenium, iodine, and cobalt are three examples. If not present in the soil, these elements must be added to animal (or human) food as a supplement.

Because of the mysteries still unsolved in the realm of trace elements, this frontier of soil science has become most fascinating—and most in need of imaginative young scientists with a vision broader than just formulating chemical fertilizer recipes for agribusiness. At this point, the laymen can be sure of only two generalizations about trace elements. First, most agronomists agree that a soil rich in organic matter seems to supply plants naturally with adequate amounts of most trace elements. Exceptions are copper and manganese on some heavy muck and peat soils. Otherwise, organic matter, especially from manure or compost, seems to prevent known trace element deficiencies. That's comforting to the organicist faced with a science that still has much to learn in its attempt to substitute processed chemicals for natural soil fertility and to duplicate artificially the finely-tuned balance of a healthy soil. The efficacy of organic matter to make trace elements available to plants also is a reminder to organic farmers and gardeners not to be stampeded by salesmen into buying an expensive trace element fertilizer. Nine times out of ten you won't need it.

The second generalization about trace elements on which everyone agrees is that the quantities needed are very small indeed. Just a little too much can be toxic to the plants or the animals eating them and just as harmful to the soil as a deficiency. If your alfalfa has the "yellows" due to boron deficiency, for instance, the soil probably needs only five pounds of actual boron *per acre*. If you make a mistake and apply twenty pounds, you most likely would kill the alfalfa or poison any cattle that tried to eat it. If your apple tree is suffering from internal cork disease, it needs boron, but if you sprinkle borax around the tree, remember that a little dab will do it—a couple of spoonfuls is enough!

The sensitiveness of plants to boron is nothing compared to molybdenum. Requirements are measured in ounces per acre. A few ounces too much and the plants could be toxic to animals grazing them. Selenium is an even better example. It must be present in soil in a quantity of only 0.1 to 0.3 parts per million, or animals eating grains or pasture crops grown on it will sicken. But in amounts over three parts per million in cattle feed, selenium can be toxic!

The first deduction to make from these examples is that you'd better know what you're doing if you decide to apply special trace element fertilizers to your soil. It is far safer for the organicist to rely on the natural workings of organic matter or the trace elements found in various rock mineral fertilizers, which we'll get to a little later. Secondly, the critical levels at which some elements must be present in the soil, together with the delicate balance that must be maintained between them and other elements so that all of them will be available to plants in proper amounts, form a powerful argument for the healthfulness of organically grown food. How can those agricultural practitioners, whose idea of soil enrichment is to heap on the chemical nitrogen, phosphorus, and potash, be so sure that organically grown food is no more nutritious than chemically grown? Science just doesn't know enough yet about the functions of trace elements for anyone to know—either way. Who can be so cocksure he can duplicate in the laboratory the action and reaction of the elements in well-managed soil of high organic content, when he admittedly hasn't discovered all the facts yet? I think of the remarks of Dr. Roger Williams, discoverer of the B vitamin, pantothenic acid, pointing out that most of us now understand the necessity to our health of iron, calcium, and iodine, but have not been educated yet to realize that other elements like manganese, copper, zinc, and molybdenum are also essential to healthy life. Williams wrote in *Texas Monthly,* August 1974:

> *Our knowledge of how to nourish our individual*
> *selves so that we will live out our full life spans*
> *in good health is abysmally inadequate. And we*
> *can't even get this information from our doctor*
> *because nutrition is not studied seriously in medi-*

cal schools. And the committees and commissions who are supposed to be environmental experts are blank when it comes to our food environment.

Chelation

Another discovery in soil science promises to shed more light on trace elements and especially trace metal fertility in the soil. Organic matter is known not only to provide trace elements to plants out of its own humus, but through a process called chelation, it can also make available to plants more trace metals already in the soil. Soil science has assumed for a long time that plants can use nutrients only in soluble form. The efficacy of chemical fertilizers has been measured largely in the degree of water solubility, which is much higher than that of organic materials. But it seems that organic "chelators"—whether natural ones in the soil or commercial ones applied to the soil—can clamp onto ions of metals and entrap them within organic molecules. Then the whole complex of inorganic metal and organic molecule can be taken up by the plant. Dr. Albert Schatz in *Compost Science* says:

> *It is paradoxical that so much effort has been devoted in recent years to a few synthetic chelates while the vast reservoir of natural products, literally at our feet, still arouses far less interest. . . . Our thinking has been colored by the classical view of soils which differentiates between organic and inorganic matter. This has caused us to neglect what may well be the most important constituents in soils: namely their organic-metal chelates. What is needed now is not merely a regrouping of facts or a reclassification of information but in effect a philosophically new approach to soil science. For the future lies with the naturally occurring chelates in the soils themselves.*

The noted soil scientist William Albrecht already in the 1950s stressed the importance of natural chelation occurring in soils rich in organic matter. He noted rather wryly that man had finally discovered in the laboratory what nature had been doing all along, fixing an inorganic ion within a larger organic molecule for better nutrient uptake.

The commercially available chelator most commonly used is called EDTA for ethylene-diamine tetraacetic acid. It works, but as Albrecht (and other experimenters) observe, no better than natural chelators. In one experiment EDTA promptly cleared up a case of iron chlorosis, but more significant was the additional demonstration adding water leachings from a highly organic soil in place of the manufactured EDTA. This natural substitute mobilized the iron to cure the chlorosis just as the EDTA did.

There are many examples of chelation in both biological and botanical functions. The magnesium used in a plant in the process of producing chlorophyll is chelated. The iron in our blood is present in a chelated form. As Schatz says:

> Men took advantage of the chelating action of organic matter long before science could explain the chemistry involved. One example is the use of manure to enhance plant growth. This beneficial effect was for a long time attributed to the minerals that were returned to the soil. But that is only part of the explanation. Many organic substances formed by decomposing manure are excellent chelating agents whose most important function is to make trace metals available for higher plants.

The chelating power of organic compounds explains why manure and rock phosphate give better fertility together than when applied separately. The chelators in the manure make the nutrients in the phosphates more available.

Following is a list of the most important trace elements (as far as we know now), together with some signs on how to spot deficiencies and what to do about them. Keep these shortages in perspective as you read. Deficiencies are not critical yet, except in specific instances or areas, usually on soils of somewhat marginal fertility to begin with. Just remember: *The first thing you should do, if you spot an apparent deficiency, is to have your soil tested by a reputable laboratory.*

Zinc

Of all the micronutrients, cases of zinc shortages in the soil are probably the most widespread. Deficiency is being reported even on some rich cornbelt land that has been intensely farmed with high chemical fertilizer rates. "We used to think that if we applied adequate amounts of NPK, our micronutrient content in the soil would take care of itself, but not any more," a midwestern agricultural consultant told me. "With intensive cropping and significantly higher yields, the small quantities of micronutrients available naturally aren't always enough now." The problem is, however, more a matter of too much NPK in relation to available zinc rather than a real zinc deficiency. But it raises the question of whether food so produced without supplemental zinc is as healthful as it should or could be.

Zinc deficiency is apt to show up on alkaline farmland west of the Mississippi on soils of comparatively low natural fertility. This is true especially where land leveling for irrigation purposes has removed topsoil. If you are gardening lighter soils in states like Kansas and Nebraska you could have the same problem where bulldozers have removed topsoil for landscaping purposes.

Even on good but hilly land, where zinc is generally in adequate supply, badly eroded areas could be suffering from a deficiency. I recently visited a farm on the extreme western edge of Iowa where this kind of zinc deficiency had occurred. Corn on the zinc deficient parts of the fields looked weak and pale despite heavy NPK applications. White streaks on the corn leaves and an almost white pallor to all the green parts of the corn plants indicated zinc deficiency. An annual application of two pounds of actual zinc per acre in dry form, or a gallon in liquid form per acre, mixed with the rest of the fertilizer, cured the problem. Since two pounds is very little when spread over an acre, the mixing of the fertilizers must be left to the most careful and expert custom applicators.

In apple trees (and pecans) zinc deficiency shows up as a disease called apple rosette. The tips of branches grow terminal whorls of unusually small leaves. For about six to eight inches below this terminal whorl, the

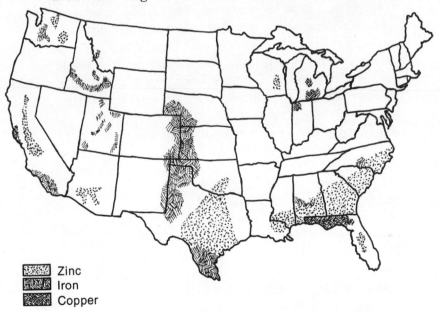

Zinc
Iron
Copper

Areas in which copper, iron, molybdenum, and zinc deficiencies occur, as revealed by limited growth or other symptoms of nutritional troubles in specific crops. The general areas shown are actually intermittent in character.

branch may drop all leaves. Sometimes a clutch of new twigs will grow out below the bare part of the branch, but these leaves will become mottled and malformed. In Florida and California, zinc deficiency will result in similar symptoms on peach trees. Peach tree leaves will also become excessively crinkled and chlorotic, but these symptoms resemble those of quite a few other diseases and are of very little diagnostic help for ordinary gardeners like you and me. That's true of many symptoms of trace element deficiency.

In vegetables, squash seems most prone to zinc deficiency, though reported cases are not numerous. One symptom is brown spots on the leaves. Zinc-deficient potatoes may contain brown spots, too. Sweet corn, like field corn, may show white specks on the leaves, or what growers call "white bud."

Manure is by far the best organic way to maintain proper zinc levels in your garden soil. Soil experts of whatever persuasion agree that well-manured fields have not been found to be zinc deficient. Raw phosphate rock contains traces of zinc too. Zinc sulfate is the common commercial fertilizer to apply when zinc is needed, but most organicists have strong reservations about sulfate fertilizers, as explained in the preceding chapter.

The importance of zinc in plant nutrition can hardly be overemphasized when we look at recent discoveries in animal and human nutrition. When corn is adequately supplied with zinc, it contains higher levels of tryptophan, as essential an amino acid as lysine. If the corn doesn't have enough zinc, it doesn't contain enough tryptophan. Remembering that soils high in organic matter maintain good zinc levels, don't let anyone tell you that organically-raised food "can't possibly" be more nutritious than its opposite.

Zinc is essential to good health in many ways. "Within the past few years, investigators have demonstrated in rapid succession that zinc deficiency is common in man and that this deficiency is a critical factor in impaired growth, delayed healing and chronic disease," stated Dr. W. J. Pories at the 1968 gathering of the American Association for the Advancement of Science, as quoted in *Prevention* magazine. Zinc seems to be important (along with calcium, of course) in the growth and development of strong bones. Some researchers think that epilepsy may be connected to a nutritional deficiency stemming from a greater than normal requirement for taurine and zinc. Zinc is necessary to maintain a normal serum vitamin A level. Poor appetite and the phenomenon called pica—eating or chewing on weird and inedible materials—may be due to zinc deficiency. And wouldn't you know, some scientists postulate that zinc might help control the common cold!

The final verdict on zinc isn't in. Whether its nutritional stature will grow even more we don't know. But I know enough to be grateful I can eat food from gardens where I've worked hard to build high levels of organic matter.

Calcium

Calcium is an important micronutrient—important enough to be called a major nutrient, in fact. Liming (which we will get to shortly) takes care of calcium deficiencies, and bone meal helps, too. No sense repeating what appears in detail in other chapters.

Boron

Boron may not be as significant to human health as zinc (though it comes in handy when you're trying to get the laundry clean), but it certainly is crucial in healthy plant growth. Boron and calcium have some kind of working relationship with each other in the soil that we don't yet know a lot about. If calcium gets too

73

high in a soil, either naturally or from heavy liming, the boron seems to become unavailable. The two elements must be kept in balance.

Boron deficiency in commercial agriculture shows up in cotton and alfalfa. Shortage in potatoes has been reported only rarely, and when growers in Maine first tried to remedy it, they commonly added too much borax and got in worse trouble. Vegetables may come up short on boron on both very light or very heavy soils, if lime has been heavily applied. Cracked stem in celery in Florida comes from boron deficiency, also brown heart disease in beets, turnips, and other root crops. If you cut through the root of a sickly plant and find the core brown and watery, that's brown heart. Cauliflower deficient in boron shows symptoms like brown heart, only the dark, watery spots appear in the stems of the cauli-

BORON DEFICIENCIES

flower head. Sweet potatoes may develop dark, water-soaked areas, scattered through the tubers, and dark cankers commonly erupt on the surface too. The sweet potato vines are stunted and those leaf branches that should grow straight up from the ground-hugging vine will be gnarled and twisted instead. Hollow stem in cabbage is caused by boron deficiency.

While we tend to think of trace element deficiencies as more characteristic of the South and West, boron deficiency in apple orchards occurs widely in the North and Northeast. As with the zinc-corn relationship, apple trees heavily fertilized with chemicals, especially nitrogen, will need more boron than normal in the soil. Deficiency exhibits itself in the form of two diseases called "internal cork" and "external cork." In internal cork, the water-soaked, dark brown lesions characteristic of boron deficiency in other plants appear throughout the flesh of the apple. In the latter stages, the lesions dry and become corky—hence the name. Internal cork may appear from about two weeks after the fruit first forms on the trees until the apples are mature.

External cork is similar, and in fact both diseases may occur together. The lesions appear only on the surface of the apples in external cork early in the growing season, when the apples are ping-pong ball size. The lesions cause cracking and wrinkling of the fruit, rendering it unmarketable even if it hangs on the tree and matures. Don't confuse these symptoms with similar ones caused by the much more common fungus disease, apple scab. In severe boron shortages, branch tips lose their leaves and die back. The whole tree will eventually die if the deficiency is not remedied.

Organically managed soils seldom show boron deficiency once organic matter content is above 3 percent. Ordinary household borax can be used in a pinch. A pinch is about right, too—four to five ounces per 1,000 square feet. Granite dust is a safer source of boron.

Magnesium

Without magnesium, no chlorophyll in plants; no chlorophyll, goodbye everything. Fortunately, we don't have to worry about how the plant uses the magnesium for making chlorophyll or for that matter how it gets the stuff from the ground. Nature has the process well in hand. All we have to do is make sure enough magnesium remains available in the soil to keep the process going.

Fortunately, that's not usually difficult. Only very small amounts are necessary, all of which can be provided by the use of dolomitic limestone to lime your soil. This kind of limestone contains a good supply. Raw rock phosphate contains some magnesium, too. In those rare cases where your soil is already alkaline and you don't want to use limestone at all, there are organic magnesium chelates available from specialized fertilizer dealers. Only experts should apply them. Seeds and grains con-

MAGNESIUM AND MANGANESE DEFICIENCIES

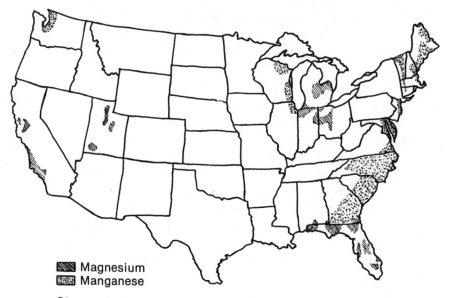

▨ Magnesium
▨ Manganese

tain a relatively high percentage of magnesium. Because of the magnesium in chlorophyll, decomposed plant leaves will contain the nutrient also.

A slight deficiency of magnesium may result in no clear symptoms at all; severe shortages cause paling or streaking of plant leaves similar to other problems. Visual identification of magnesium deficiency is very difficult, even for experts. An imbalance of magnesium in the diets of grazing cattle causes grass tetany. This disease is becoming more common in central and southern states.[10]

Americans are prone to magnesium deficiency. We eat bread that does not contain the wheat germ, where most of the magnesium is found. We boil the magnesium out of our vegetables and throw the water away. We eat lots of dairy products which contain little magnesium, and few raw seeds, nuts, and whole grains that are rich in magnesium. In a June 1964 article, "The Requirement of Magnesium by the Normal Adult," in *The Journal of Clinical Nutrition,* Mildred S. Seelig, M.D., writes that low magnesium intake "is dangerous for the nervous system, heart and kidneys . . ." and "a prolonged dietary deficiency may contribute to the development of chronic disease."

J. I. Rodale wrote about an interesting test he conducted at his experimental farm concerning the connection between high organic matter in the soil and magnesium: "I have recently concluded an experiment on our farm with two groups of chickens, fed since they were a day old. One group was fed with organically produced food grown on our farm. The other group was fed on purchased mash. Later on, some eggs laid by each group were analyzed by a reputable laboratory (La Wall and Harrison in Philadelphia), and it was found that all the eggs laid by the organic group had 100 percent more magnesium than the eggs of the other chickens."

Iron

Plants need very little iron, but that little bit they need very much. There's actually a lot of iron in most soils, around twenty tons per acre in the form of iron oxide in the first eight inches. But very little of this is available to the plant. Neutral or alkaline soils especially tend to "lock up" the iron. The chlorosis that then affects the plants is often called "lime sickness." The disease seems to be especially prevalent if excessive amounts of soluble phosphates have been added to soil in the above condition.

Iron chlorosis is not an uncommon nutritional deficiency of plants, though the exact relationship between the iron and the affected chlorophyll is not presently understood. Healthy plants need about two pounds of available iron per acre which the mildly acidifying action of decaying organic matter can provide in most cases. Glauconite or greensand is a good supplemental source of iron for organic soil.

According to researchers at Texas A & M, foliar spray applications of iron are generally more effective than soil-applied iron, especially on alkaline soils. The opposite is true for correction of other micronutrient shortages.

Recent surveys indicate that anemia caused by iron deficient diets is becoming common among young women and infants in this country, according to nutritionists at Purdue University. They cite lack of exercise leading to loss of appetite and possible deficiencies of iron in our modern, fabricated foods as the reasons. Beans, meat, whole wheat foods, greens, and prunes from soil with sufficient iron in it are safe, effective remedies.

Sulfur

Sulfur quite possibly should be called a major nutrient rather than a minor one. There's more of it in some plants than phosphorus. The awful smell of rotting cabbage comes from the sulfur in the plant. In oxidized form, sulfur combines commonly in the soil with other elements to form sulfates: calcium sulfate (gypsum), potassium sulfate, ammonium sulfate, zinc sulfate.

Sulfur and sulfur compounds have been dismissed summarily by organicists as unacceptable for purposes of organic gardening and farming. Even though sulfur exists in deposits as natural as some other approved soil supplements, the reasons for this stand [see page 61] are commendable. However, as the science of organic agriculture progresses, there will no doubt be controversy over this point among organicists. At least I hope so; I'd hate to think the organic method was already cut and dried less than fifty years from its inception. With some assurance I can predict a good argument for the following reasons: 1) Sulfur is necessary for plant growth as well as animal health. 2) Wherever sulfur-containing fuels are burned (which is just about everywhere now), rain washes from the atmosphere back into the ground an adequate amount of sulfur—about ten pounds per acre annually. 3) Therefore, by strictest definition, organically grown foods are an impossibility wherever sulfur from burned fuels rises into the atmosphere.[11]

Besides this, at least we do not have to worry much about sulfur deficiency. Where it has been observed, the principal symptom is yellowing of the leaves, which can be distinguished from nitrogen deficiency because the leaves don't completely dry up as they do in the latter situation. If you must have a more "natural" sulfur than that found in natural deposits, I suggest using sulfur water like that found in so many wells in the East and Midwest. The water on the farm where I live is so high in sulfur that I'm sure a watering or two with it on the garden would more than fill any annual need the ground would have for sulfur.

Manganese

Manganese serves as a sort of catalyst in the plant. To oversimplify, it "directs" other nutrients coming into the plant to their proper stations where they can carry out their functions. In the soil, manganese seems to assist legumes in the process of nitrogen fixation. Soil needs only a very small amount of manganese—less than a pound per acre to produce a 100 bushel per acre corn crop.

A deficiency becomes evident in a general yellowing of leaves, visually indistinguishable from symptoms of several other deficiencies. I've seen manganese deficiency, or what the experts diagnosed as that, in commercial soybean fields that had been intensely farmed and fertilized with chemicals. The yellow discoloration occurred in small patches throughout the field and looked the way beans do when growing on poorly-drained, low spots in clay ground. But no moisture problem was apparent in these cases. In fact, one field had received very little rain that summer. Bush and pole beans will be similarly affected. In fact, most vegetables will get yellow leaves except beets, which instead take on a deep purplish-red hue.

High organic matter content alone will not assure proper manganese levels all the time. Manganese sulfate is one commercial fertilizer that will correct a deficiency. The organic grower should first check his soil pH. Manganese shortage will occur in a high organic soil when the soil is too alkaline, as from excessive liming. Omit the lime for a couple of years at least and work into the soil more acid kinds of organic matter like oak leaves.

Copper

Copper, like manganese, is a trace metal that you can't depend on organic matter to provide. In fact, certain types of heavy muck and peat soils high in organic content sometimes lack sufficient copper. Elsewhere, the problem is quite minor. On these muck soils, lettuce leaves lose their crispy firmness and may turn pale. Tomato leaves discolor to a deep blue-green and also develop the characteristic lack of firmness. Onion leaves, in addition, may become partially covered with yellow scale.

Copper sulfate is the traditional nonorganic fertilizer to correct the problem. Organicists can sometimes remedy the situation with sawdust or wood shavings. Bluegrass contains copper, and so grass clippings would help too. Brome grass is also comparatively high in copper—as are seeds of all kinds.

MINERAL DEFICIENCIES

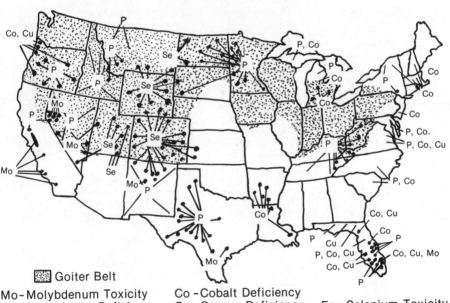

Goiter Belt

Mo- Molybdenum Toxicity   Co -Cobalt Deficiency
P — Phosphorus Deficiency   Cu - Copper Deficiency   Fe – Selenium Toxicity

Known areas in the United States where mineral-nutritional diseases of animals occur. The dots indicate approximate locations where troubles occur.

81

TRACE MINERALS

Trace Minerals	Hunger Signs	Accumulator Plants and Other Sources
Boron	Dwarfing of alfalfa, heart rot of beets, corking of apples, stem cracking in celery, discoloration of cauliflower	Vetch Sweet clover Muskmelon leaves Granite dust Agricultural frit
Cobalt	Anemia, muscular atrophy, depraved appetite, poor growth	Vetch Most legumes Kentucky bluegrass Peach tree refuse Basic rocks
Copper	Paralysis, anemia, falling in animals; poor growth, dwarfing of tomatoes, dieback of citrus trees or plants	Redtop Bromegrass Spinach Tobacco Dandelions Kentucky bluegrass Lignin (wood shavings, sawdust) Agricultural frit
Iron	Anemia, salt sickness in animals, chlorosis in plants	Many weeds Seaweed
Manganese	Poor milk production, deformity of hogs, poultry; poor growth, chlorosis of tomatoes, gray speck of oats and peas, poor leaf color in plants	Forest leaf mold (especially hickory, white oak) Alfalfa Carrot tops Redtop Bromegrass
Molybdenum	Hair loss, skin thickening in animals; poor fruiting, dieback in citrus, white bud in corn, top blight of some nut trees	Cornstalks Vetch Ragweed, Horsetail Poplar and hickory leaves; Peach tree clippings Agricultural frit
Zinc	Necrosis of leaf edges	Vetch Alfalfa Agricultural frit Rock phosphate

Molybdenum

A relatively new discovery as an essential micronutrient (the 1940s), molybdenum is needed in very small quantities. Natural shortages are rare, but have been induced in greenhouse culture. Sodium molybdate solution brushed on the leaves corrected the situation. Molybdenum may be more of a problem in surplus rather than deficiency. As a pollutant in industrial smoke, molybdenum is thought to be the culprit in some cases of plant and animal poisoning.

Cobalt

Curiously, cobalt does not seem to be necessary for healthy plant growth, but must be present in plants for the health of animals eating them. Without cobalt, cows become scruffy and emaciated. The condition clears up if the cattle are fed a cobalt supplement or moved to pastures where the soil has sufficient quantities of this element. Fortunately, cobalt deficiency is very rare.

Chlorine

Extremely small amounts of this micronutrient are necessary, too. No one bothers much with chlorine deficiency for a very simple reason: rain supplies the soil with all it needs.

To sum up: garden organically and you'll rarely have a trace element problem. Before you decide you do have such a problem, get soil tests run at a reputable laboratory. Don't rely on visual diagnoses.

Chapter 6

Organic Matter and Humus: Lifeblood of the Soil

We experienced a severe drought in Ohio a few years ago. By the middle of July both gardens and fields showed badly stunted and shriveled crops. There's no joy in walking such fields, but I did it more than once that summer. Rarely in a lifetime does one get a chance to view corn under so much stress. (I hope!) Rarely can the value of organic matter in the soil be so easily observed.

A typical field in this generally fertile farmland of northern Ohio looks comparatively flat to an outsider or a traveller on the highway—especially if he comes from more mountainous areas. Those of us who have farmed this land know its flatness is deceiving. The topography of the land is gently rolling, and even where this undulation may not be sharply defined, the type of soil is. In a distance of no more than twenty-five feet, ascending a height of no more than three feet, you can walk from a very black rich soil to a light tan not-so-rich soil on the higher elevation. The blackness is the coloring organic matter gives to the former. Its disappearance from the high ground is the result of at least one hundred years of intensive cultivation and erosion.

In a good year, when rainfall is adequate, the tan soils produce almost as well as the black soils if heavily laced with fertilizers, but under stress the chemicals aren't much help. On the tan ground that droughty summer, the corn was dying—it grew about a foot tall. On the black ground just a few feet away, the corn stalks were head-high. The difference was almost as graphic as a picture of desert beside tropical jungle. Yet the entire field was fertilized, planted, cultivated, and chemicalized in exactly the same manner. The difference, of course, was the extra moisture in the black ground, *retained there by the organic matter in the soil.* One couldn't even say the lower ground was moister because of run-off from the higher ground for there had been no run-off since that ground was plowed and planted. It hadn't rained enough.

Walking through the corn in a field I had not visited before, I found even better proof of the value of organic matter. (I must continue finding evidence, you understand, because while some champions of modern farming admit that many farms are being depleted of organic matter, they don't think it matters very much.) Whereas the difference in the growth of the corn I have described previously could be considered only a difference of soil type, I found myself looking at shriveled corn next to still healthy corn all on the tan soil on an elevation of several acres' size. You could divide the good corn from the poor with a ruler, and the difference ran at right angles to the rows, so the explanation was not some mechanical failure of the planter.

I examined the ground under the corn. What had happened seemed obvious, and subsequent checking proved my guess correct. A fence had previously divided that field where now poor and good corn grew. But the land where the good corn grew had been cleared to the plow only relatively recently, while the other field had been intensely cultivated for years. The soil where the better corn grew hadn't had all the organic matter cultivated out of it!

Few whole fields of corn in this area were growing near normal that year. When I found one, invariably the field belonged to a livestock farmer, was in sod or clover the previous year, and had been fertilized that spring with manure. The same observation held true of gardens. Where composts, manures, and mulches had been used in the past, the vegetables were producing almost normally. Gardens with a history of only chemical fertilizer were simply, sadly, withering away.

What Organic Matter Is

What is this precious stuff, organic matter? Technically, anything with carbon in it is "organic" but for purposes of improving soil, we exclude by definition many "organic" materials that would actually be harmful to plants. Oil, for instance, is organic but you wouldn't want to pour it on your garden. Organic matter for improving soil consists of any once-living plant or animal material that will decompose into humus: dead plants, bugs, and animals large, small, and microscopic; manure, straw, hay, leaves, grass clippings, roots, flesh, hair, and so forth.

As organic matter decomposes in the soil it provides many marvelous benefits: 1) Feeds the microorganisms without which we would not have soil. 2) Helps make available the nutrients that are in the soil, breaking down plant food to forms plants can eat. 3) Improves the tilth of soil, so your garden is easier to cultivate.

4) Aerates soil so plants don't suffocate. 5) Gives soil a crumbly texture that retains moisture—makes sandy soil hold together better and clay soil crumble apart better. 6) Aids soil to resist water and wind erosion for the same reason.[12] 7) Causes soil to warm up faster in spring, by darkening its color. 8) Allows man to produce food with fewer expenditures of natural resources and fossil fuels. 9) Gives food better quality and higher nutrient content.

That last advantage is disputed, but ask an unprejudiced eater—a cow. Grazing animals invariably eat the grass from an uncultivated fence row where organic matter is high before eating from a field where intense cultivation has depleted organic matter. And if you think a watermelon raised on sandy soil solely on the strength of chemical fertilizer won't taste much less sweet than one raised over a bushel of rotten manure—sunlight being equal—then you just ain't lived yet, as my granddaddy would say. But even better evidence is that in Florida, land developers followed the traditional practice for years of putting newly cleared land into watermelons. After a couple of crops used up the nutrients in that new soil, the melons didn't do so well and then the developers would plant houses instead.

For a gardener who hopes to have plenty to eat in the world of tomorrow, he'd better make plans to raise it himself, building humus in his garden soil from the decay of organic matter.[13] Should the day come when water (let alone food) becomes an expensive commodity, or fuel becomes too dear to use in garden tractors and tillers, or you can't afford chemicals even if you wanted them, or can't even afford to haul in extra organic fertilizers, a soil already enriched will tide you through a crisis that money could not. And of course, if everyone improved his soil to a 5 percent organic matter content, there would be no crisis.

In the Garden

One of the most interesting accounts of how valuable organic matter is to a garden was reported by a New York banker and avid gardener, Hugh Ward, in a publication of the Brooklyn Botanic Garden, of which he was a member. Ward kept close records over a period of six years of the chemical content and organic matter of his garden plots. Before he began cultivating these plots organically, the sandy Long Island soil showed a content of 120 pounds of phosphorus per acre, 150 pounds of potash, and ten pounds of nitrogen. The first year he applied composted organic matter at the rate of twenty tons per acre, rototilled immediately to a depth of six inches. Each year thereafter, he applied the compost at the rate of ten tons per acre. The compost was formed out of successive six-inch layers of vegetable matter and one-inch layers of chicken manure with a sprinkling of topsoil, limestone, and rock phosphate on each layer.

At the end of the first year, analysis showed a phosphorus content of 680 pounds per acre, potash 300 pounds, nitrogen twenty pounds. At the end of the second year, phosphorus was 710 pounds per acre, potash 372 pounds, and nitrogen 100 pounds. By then the organic matter content had risen to a respectable 3.64 percent. At the end of six years of the same treatment, phosphorus was unbelievably high at 800 pounds per acre (most likely not all of it available, coming from the rock phosphate source—you wouldn't want it to be all available), potash 450 pounds, and nitrogen forty pounds. Organic matter content had reached 5.98 percent—in that sandy soil! Significantly, Ward reported "highly successful" crops even without high nitrogen. Moreover, Ward said his soil structure was vastly improved and moisture-holding capacity substantially increased. Here is a banker who understands real wealth.

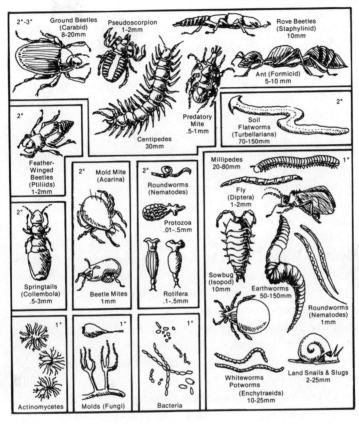

2°-3° Ground Beetles (Carabid) 8-20mm	Pseudoscorpion 1-2mm		Rove Beetles (Staphylinid) 10mm

Ant (Formicid) 5-10 mm

Predatory Mite .5-1mm

Centipedes 30mm

2° Soil Flatworms (Turbellarians) 70-150mm

2° Feather-Winged Beetles (Ptiliids) 1-2mm

2° Mold Mite (Acarina)

2° Roundworms (Nematodes)

Millipedes 20-80mm 1°

Fly (Diptera) 1-2mm

Protozoa .01-.5mm

2° Springtails (Collembola) .5-3mm

Beetle Mites 1mm

Rotifera .1-.5mm

Sowbug (Isopod) 10mm

Earthworms 50-150mm

Roundworms (Nematodes) 1mm

1° Actinomycetes

1° Molds (Fungi)

1° Bacteria

Whiteworms Potworms (Enchytraeids) 10-25mm

Land Snails & Slugs 2-25mm

FOOD WEB OF THE COMPOST PILE

1° = First Level Consumers
2° = Second Level Consumers
3° = Third Level Consumers

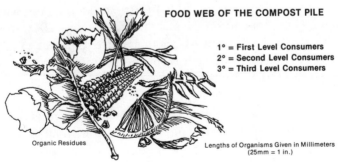

Organic Residues

Lengths of Organisms Given in Millimeters (25mm = 1 in.)

Organic gardeners report successes like that every year, even though they rarely have such detailed records to support their claims. Wherever organic matter in quantity has been added to soil *for a fairly long period of time,* it seems to give results greater than the sum of its parts. Two hundred pounds per acre of commercial fertilizer with high nitrogen, phosphorus and potash (NPK) content is far more "potent," at least mathematically, than fifteen tons of manure. A ton of manure will have only about ten pounds of nitrogen in it, for example. But the manure will give a growth response lasting much longer than the inorganic fertilizer. This is partly because the nitrogen in commercial fertilizer is soluble in water and becomes available very quickly to plants, unlike the nitrogen in the manure.

But that doesn't explain the whole story to my satisfaction. Why, I want to know, do commercial farmers have to keep increasing the rate of inorganic fertilizer applications in order to maintain high yields, while organic growers find it is possible (sometimes even necessary) to reduce applications of manure and other organic materials without affecting yields? In any case, organic yields invariably keep going up without increasing the rate of application beyond the optimum level. A field fertilized with fifteen tons of manure per acre for ten consecutive years will continue to produce well for three more years without any added fertilizer at all. And why not? The population of bacteria in the soil is related directly to the amount of organic matter present. Some bacteria convert nitrogen from the air to a form plants can use. Other bacteria convert natural ammonia into nitrates available for plant growth.

I think that the artificial NPK being applied is more than adequate to maintain yields, but without a concomitant increase in organic matter and therefore in the microorganisms that feed on the organic matter, the growing plants simply don't have the capacity to absorb all the fertilizer. Also, soils high in organic matter protect soil microorganisms from overdoses of pesticides through a phenomenon called "organic shielding." [14]

Moreover, soil high in organic matter has proven itself capable of controlling some soil-borne diseases. Rye plowed down controls potato scab; that's one long-known example. More recently, Indian scientists have clearly demonstrated the effectiveness of organic soil amendments in controlling nematodes.[15]

Life in the Soil

One of the most unfortunate accidents of language in modern times is the equating of soil and dirt with the notion of defilement. The soil is not dirty, it is not unclean, it is not of itself productive of disease. It produces life. It *is* life. The soil is as alive as the teeming center of the city—more so. Every acre of land contains such quantities of microscopic life that despite their individual size, they weigh together as much as 800 pounds. Algae, bacteria, fungi, actinomycetes live and die in the soil by the billions.[16] Life-giving antibiotics like streptomycin and terramycin come from actinomycetes living naturally

AVERAGE NUMBER OF SOIL MICROFLORA AND THEIR LIVE WEIGHT PER ACRE TO PLOW DEPTH		
Group	Average Number per Gram of Soil	Live Weight per Acre to Plow Depth (Pounds)
Bacteria	1 billion	500
Actinomycetes	10 million	750
Fungi	1 million	1000
Algae	100 thousand	150
Total	—	2400

91

in the dirt. They're grown in laboratory cultures now because we need large quantities handy. Perhaps there is so much need for antibiotics because careless treatment of the soil prevents a proper natural supply of these disease fighters from getting into our plants, animals, and ourselves. I'm convinced that scours in baby calves is much more of a problem today than it was even when I was a kid raising calves. Today it is difficult to raise calves at all without administering commercially available antibiotics. Why? Who knows; we may have traded a natural process for an artificial and vastly more expensive one.[17]

So far, scientists have learned to use only a few of hundreds of known antibiotic–producing organisms living naturally in the soil. How much good are the "unknowns" doing us already? Who wants to gamble them away by destroying the soil's natural balance? Some kinds of bacteria in the soil produce hormones and vitamins. Such bacteria are the *sole* present source of vitamin B-12, which prevents anemia.

Evidence exists that when humus is plentiful, micromolds and other microorganisms perform a sort of natural sanitation job—they reduce the number of harmful fungi and plant pathogens.[18] Minute animals as well as plants grow in the soil: protozoa, insects, worms. How many good ones are killed in order to poison one harmful species?

In a thimbleful of soil there are an estimated 100,000 protozoa, two billion bacteria, thirty million fungal plants. Microbiologists say that under a microscope a vast, awesome world of great beauty opens up to them— a world absolutely fundamental to our existence. A drop of poison chemical to that world may be as devastating as an atomic bomb to a city.[19] No wonder microbiologists so often are in close agreement with organicists. Perhaps we all should spend more time looking at the world through a microscope.

Getting Humus Into the Soil

Organic matter breaks down—rots—into humus and it is the process itself, as much as the organic matter or the humus that should get the credit for the benefits I've mentioned.[20] You can produce humus by composting organic matter in a heap, or by spreading the organic matter as "sheet compost" directly on the land, where it slowly rots away and the humus is absorbed into the earth. Or you can plow organic matter into the soil mechanically with spade, rotary tiller, plow, or disk. Each of these activities—composting, sheet composting or mulching, and cultivation—will be treated in detail in subsequent chapters. Suffice it to say here that if you follow the organic methods of composting and mulching you will provide your ground with adequate organic matter. The problem is finding enough organic materials. Here are a few of the common, more easily obtainable materials.

Leaves

Tree leaves that fall in autumn probably are the city and suburban gardeners' best source of organic matter. Especially now that so many local ordinances ban leaf burning, you should have no trouble finding a supply. Where the leaves are put in plastic bags for the garbage man or the city to pick up, you can haul them in truck or trailer to your property. I know one gardener who gets paid for hauling leaves! You can form compost heaps with them, or spread them a foot deep directly on your garden or around ornamentals and trees, as I do. Often, I keep the leaves bagged over winter and spread them after the soil warms up in early summer.

Some towns clean up leaves with giant vacuum hoses that suck them into trucks. In the process, the leaves get shredded somewhat, too. If you can arrange to have these leaves hauled to your property, they are better than hand-raked ones. The shredding packs more leaf to the square foot and allows them to rot into humus quicker.

Grass Clippings

Suburbanites are also packing lawn clippings in plastic bags for the garbage man, handy for you, too. It's best to spread fresh clippings on soil as mulch right away. If they stand in a plastic bag, they heat and smell terrible. In the compost heap, spread fresh clippings in shallow layers, no more than four inches thick. Dry clippings are like hay and won't heat badly unless they get wet.

Leaves belong in your garden. Don't burn them, don't bag them. Do collect them whenever you can find them, and spread them as a mulch throughout your garden.

Mulching with hay or straw is an easy, albeit expensive, way to boost the organic matter content of garden soil. The bales break into "slabs" of just the right size for between-row use, and when spread throughout the garden make it photogenic in an extreme, a measure of its appearance. Moreover, the material will almost melt into the soil, bolstering its fertility and tilth.

Hay and Straw

These have become almost too expensive to buy for organic matter. However expensive, straw is justified if used as necessary mulch around something like strawberries. If you can find a farmer who has spoiled hay, unfit to be fed to livestock, you can often buy it reasonably. It will probably contain weed seeds but if that worries you, compost the hay. The seeds should be killed in the normal heating of a compost pile.

Manure

Animal manures are no longer easy to find—even in the country in some areas. But where a viable animal agriculture still exists—and I'm talking mostly about dairy regions where dairy farms are plentiful or where beef cattle are fattened in large lots—you should find manure. In the latter case, a regular business has sprung up in hauling the manure away from the lots to surround-

95

ing farms where it is spread—the crops grown with it being sold back to the feedlots. It's an ideal ecological and agricultural system, but you might not be able to get a pickup load for your garden so easily. On the other hand, dairymen will often sell manure to you very reasonably if you do the hauling, or they might even give it to you.

In suburban areas, you can get horse manure for free if you do the loading and hauling. Horse owners often have comparatively small space for their animals and getting rid of the manure is problem No. 1 for them. You are solution No. 1, if you don't mind getting some exercise with a pitchfork.

For fertilizing value, manures vary not only by species of animal but by manner in which the manure is stored before use. We'll discuss that in detail later. Considered strictly as organic matter, different manures have about the same value at the same stage of decomposition. Rotted manures are more valuable than fresh because the change to humus is already well advanced in the former. Nitrogen in rotted manures won't "burn" plants, as it sometimes will in fresh manures.

Sawdust and Shredded Bark

If you live close to a sawmill, you can usually get sawdust free for the hauling. Rotted sawdust is an excellent amendment to improve organic matter content. If you use fresh sawdust, you may need to add extra nitrogen with it, as the sawdust (or any organic material) will use soil nitrogen in its rotting process. That nitrogen is not lost to the soil, however; it's only borrowed for awhile. After the organic material has rotted, the nitrogen is again available to the plants.

Close to where I live is a logging operation that converts oak logs into barrel staves. The logs must be peeled first. The shredded peelings are piled into small hills where the bark composts, providing gardeners and greenhouse growers for miles around with an excellent mulch and soil amendment. Because oak wood (and leaves) tend to acidify the soil a little, I sprinkle lime on the shredded bark, except around acid-loving plants.

Vegetable Wastes

Cider mills aren't exactly common anymore, but if you live near one, you should investigate whether the pomace is available—pomace is the apple pulp after the juice has been squeezed out of it. Pomace is fairly high in phosphorus, besides being beneficial as organic matter.

If you live where sugar beets are refined—a fairly limited area—beet wastes will make a good source of organic matter. Farmers have been utilizing these wastes by making silage for cattle out of them, but you shouldn't have trouble getting a truckload or two.

Corncobs

Cobs aren't as plentiful around feed mills and grain elevators now that corn harvesters shell the corn and leave the cobs in the field. Cobs left over from sweet corn processing are often fed to cattle too. But if there's a sweet corn cannery near you, or a feed mill that still shells ear corn, you might find a steady source of corncobs for organic material for your garden. I recently

PRINCIPAL PLANT NUTRIENTS IN SAWDUST, WHEAT STRAW, ALFALFA HAY, AND SEWAGE SLUDGE IN POUNDS PER TON OF DRY MATERIAL					
Organic Material	Nitrogen (N)	Phosphorus (P)	Potassium (K)	Calcium ($CaCO_3$)	Magnesium ($MgCO_3$)
Sawdust	4	2	4	11	1
Wheat straw	10	3	12	7	2
Alfalfa hay	48	10	28	50	15
Digested sludge	48	54	Trace	—	—
Activated sludge	112	114	Trace	—	—

picked strawberries from a patch mulched with corn cobs. The berries were as clean as if ripened on straw.

Seaweed

Gardeners handy to the ocean can sometimes collect seaweed for mulch. Inland, many fresh-water ponds become clogged after a number of years with algae and other seaweed-like plants. It's no harder to scoop out a pickup load by hand than it is to fork a load of manure. We used to wade out and rake up the stuff by the handful into rowboats just to get rid of it. What an excellent source of organic matter we could have been making good use of.

For coastal dwelling gardeners, seaweed is an excellent material to use in the garden, either composted or as a mulch. Usually it can be had free for the taking. Seaweed is increasingly being used to prepare commercial organic fertilizers, an indication of its value.

Other Sources

Peat, salt hay, peat moss, buckwheat hulls, citrus waste, cotton gin trash, rice hulls, beeswing chaff from corn drying operations, tobacco stalks, cocoa bean shells, and other products of specialized industries make good sources of organic matter, but you will most often have to buy these. That usually limits you to a small amount for a special purpose. But anytime you can get these materials in quantity cheap, don't pass up the chance.

Sewage sludge may become the most reliable source of organic matter for the gardener, where it isn't already. Air-dried digested sludge can be used safely on lawns, around ornamentals, or worked into soils for food crops to be grown the following year. It should not be put around vegetables that are to be eaten raw. Heat-dried sludge is safe for all fertilizer users, say the experts, because of the destructive action of the heat upon harmful bacteria. With these few precautions, gardeners have been using sludge for years with success.[21]

Probably the most efficient way to increase organic matter in the soil in terms of energy and fuel cost is through green manures—special grass or legume crops plowed into the soil where they grow. For the organic gardener or farmer, green manuring is, I believe, the most essential management tool to success. I'll try to show why in a following chapter.

Chapter 7

How to Manage Water In and On Your Soil

It is futile to talk about maintaining or building a fertile, organic soil in your garden until you can provide the proper amount—neither too much nor too little— of water. You will have to drain your soil if it is too wet, or irrigate it if it is to dry. Even if you are lucky enough to have deep, naturally well-drained soil and abundant rainfall, you must strive by good management to conserve that abundance for periods of summer drought and protect that deep soil from erosion during periods of wet weather.

Drainage

Almost every gardener who has ever wielded a sprinkler can readily understand the need for irrigation at times, but few grasp the fact that land in the U.S., especially east of the Mississippi, more often needs drainage than it needs irrigation. Drainage usually conjures up a vision of ditching water from dank swamps and turning that land into cornfields. Or if one is knowledgeable about the dependency of wild life (and ultimately man himself) on swampland, drainage evokes nightmares of bulldozers rooting up and destroying the last vestiges of wilderness for some half-baked money-making scheme of men. Soil drainage may entail projects like that, and unfortunately often has in the past, but the kind of drainage I speak of is a gentler operation, one of primary benefit to any soil that is not well-drained naturally—and most level to gently rolling land is not. On such soils there may not be anything that resembles a swamp, yet the land, in farmer terms, "lays wet." Such soil dries out in spring only very slowly, remaining cold and wet long after crops have germinated on well-

If your proposed garden site is this wet, look for another spot. A swamp like this represents a drainage extreme. Though a swamp can, and in many cases is, drained and cultivated, it is best left the way it is.

drained soil. Then after you finally manage to get that soil planted and are lucky enough to obtain adequate germination and growth, hot dry summer weather arrives. Poorly drained soil then promptly dries up. Roots of your vegetables have not penetrated very far into such soil because all spring the water level was high. With dry weather, the water level drops drastically and your plants wilt or turn yellow. Aeration too is poor in wet land, and the soil becomes harder and more compact the more you try to cultivate it. You aggravate this condition if you rotary-till such ground before it is completely dried out. Rather than a finely-worked seed-

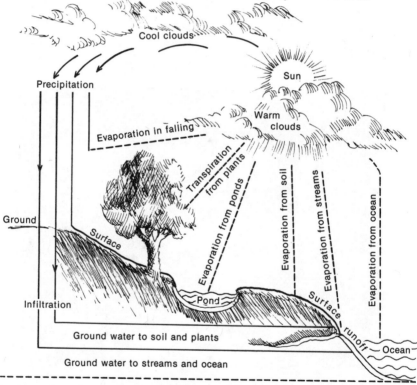

In the water cycle, the sun evaporates water from open water, the soil and plants. As it rises and forms clouds, it cools. Cooled it falls to the earth, where it maintains ground and surface water stores, feeds plants and begins again its solar-powered journey.

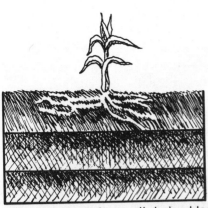

Any crop planted on well-drained land has a better chance for growth and survival. The roots of the corn at left can't penetrate the saturated soil, wet nearly to the surface. Should drought develop, the water table could easily drop to a much lower level, one that the roots couldn't reach. At right, the installation of drain tile has lowered the water level, promoting the development of deep-rooted plants.

bed, you end up with a bunch of clods. The clods, in turn, don't hold moisture crops need during drought.

The longer you try to garden wet land the more you keep on losing. In poorly drained soil plants will not make good use of plant food you apply for them. Fertilizer is merely wasted. Wet land persists in remaining acid; lime will do little good. I think the reason some people dislike gardening is because they tried it first, or were forced by circumstances to try it first, on poorly drained clay land. About all such land will produce for the gardener is a deep sense of frustration.

Underdrainage

The best way to clear up the problem in most soils is through underdrainage—placing lines of clay, cement, or plastic tile about two to three feet below the soil surface to pipe out excess water.

Visualize soil as if it were a sponge. It will "hold" or soak up a certain amount of water; any in excess of that amount either runs off, percolates down through to ground water, or waterlogs the soil. Through the

103

joints between the tiles or the perforations in the plastic type, that excess water is drawn off to an outlet—a creek, ditch, or larger tile line. City gardeners are amazed to find out that most of the level to rolling land in the eastern cornbelt is honeycombed beneath the surface with millions of feet of tile. Without it, much of that land would be next to worthless for profitable agriculture; with it, most of that land is exceedingly valuable for farming. The same truth applies to your garden.

How can you tell if you garden needs underdrainage? Are you able to cultivate the soil within forty-eight hours after an inch to inch and a half rain in June? If the ground does not dry out enough for cultivation under these circumstances until four days have elapsed, you need underdrainage. Does your ground dry out and warm enough in spring to allow you to plant as early as other gardeners in your neighborhood? Do you get 90 percent germination on early plantings? If the answer is no, you probably need underdrainage. Do your plants heave badly out of the ground over winter? That's often a sign of poorly drained land. All plantings will heave *somewhat* if left unprotected in winters with alternate freezing and thawing weather. But if *all* your strawberries are pushed out of the ground unless you absolutely bury them under mulch, the soil "lays too wet." Do your plants wilt or turn yellow during even a brief drought in summer? Do they wilt or turn yellow during a prolonged wet spell in summer? Either case will be helped immeasurably by tile drainage.

Drain Tile Systems

Tiling by hand—digging the trench out with a spade —is hard work, but not difficult. The width of the trench should be just enough to make it convenient for you to work in. Pile the dirt at the edge of the trench so it will be easy to push back in after the tile is laid. One string of four-inch tile down through most gardens will be sufficient. It will drain twenty-five feet or more on either side of it. On larger fields, the lines should go down the middle of the wet spots. If you can afford it, put a line every fifty to 100 feet in a systematic grid pattern. Get advice from the soil conservation agent in your county. He knows all about tiling and can be of immense help.

How your drainage system will be designed is governed by your outlet—the point where your water empties into a ditch, creek, or larger drain line. That's your low point, and all your tile lines must be graded to it so the water will flow out by gravity. You should have at the very least an inch of fall per 100 feet; and two or three inches are even better. A level or nearly level tile line results in slow moving water which usually causes the line to plug with dirt over a period of years. A good clay tile line properly installed will last nearly forever.

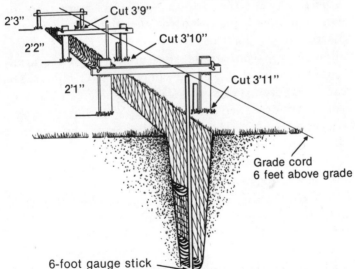

Gauge-and-line method of establishing grade for a tile drain. A cut of 3 feet 11 inches is indicated at the hub in the first station. Subtracting this cut from the length of the gauge stick (6 feet), the difference of 2 feet 1 inch is the height for setting the top of the cross bar above the hub. The gauge stick at the first station shows that the trench has been dug to the correct grade elevation at that point. The gauge stick at the second station shows that more digging is required for the needed cut of 3 feet 10 inches.

Getting an outlet often involves crossing into another property. The laws governing all such projects are well-established. Talk to county engineers, commissioners, and again your local soil conservation agent. They have the answers you need.

If just the thought of digging a tile trench by hand tires you, farm the job out. Most every community includes an operator of one of the small ditching rigs now much used to dig water and septic lines. A small tile ditcher would be even better, if one is available and the operator is willing to do a small garden job. The big tile ditchers aren't practical—they won't fit in most backyards and cost too much money.

Use common sense when you lay your tile in the trench. If using clay or cement tile (both are satisfactory; make sure they are approved by the American Standard of Testing Materials), leave a joint of about ¼ inch between tiles for the water to drain through. Most tile now being installed is continuous, perforated plastic, so you don't have to worry about joints. Don't allow sags in your grade. Be sure the tiles are firmly seated on solid earth, or they may sag after filling. You can use a level, stakes, and string to guide you and keep you on grade. (See drawing.) My grandfather used a bucket of water. Every few tiles or so, he'd pour a little water in the trench to see if it still flowed downhill like it was supposed to. He'd brag that he could tile all day on a gallon of water.

After the tiles are laid, dribble just enough dirt on and around them to cover and hold them in place. Then when you push the rest of the dirt back into the trench you don't have to worry about a clod or rock knocking a tile crooked (or breaking it). (Breakage is a problem only with cement or clay tile, not plastic tile.) If you want to make the tile work especially well the first year, or if you are in very tight clay soil, put a foot-deep layer of some organic matter over the tile before you fill in the dirt—hay, straw, etc. The tile will draw better.

Results from tile can seem almost miraculous where it was badly needed. On bare land, you can easily tell when the tile is working properly. After a rain, the soil always dries out faster directly over the tile lines, and you can see the dryness plainly. It shows up even better from an airplane, which is why aerial photos are so handy for locating old tile lines.

Sometimes, a heavy soil doesn't drain well immediately after tile installation. Drainage will improve gradually as the soil's physical condition improves, as plants grow better and put down deeper roots, thereby improving percolation.

Some clayey, jackwax soils are simply too tight for underdrainage. Water won't percolate through, or if it does, the clay particles will eventually seal over the tile so it can't drain. If this condition exists only in a well-defined wet hole, you can dig a wide hole down to the tile and fill it with stone and gravel up to within a foot of the surface. Fill in the last foot with good topsoil. Water will drain down through the gravel to the tile, and your wet spot will vanish.

Surface Drainage

Some heavy clays must be "surface-drained" because tile won't work at all in them. In such cases the land is leveled if necessary (it usually is level land al-

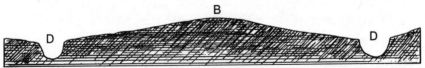

Dead furrows as drains. On tight soils, especially on fields having little slope, surface drainage may be had by plowing in narrow "lands" up and down the gentle slopes. The surface water drains from the back furrows to the dead furrows, thence down the dead furrows and off the field. B, back furrow; D, dead furrow.

ready) and then shallow ditches are shaped in the surface with enough grade to carry the water to deep ditches at the edges of the fields. The shallow ditches can be easily farmed over, and they will carry away excess surface water rather than allowing it to pond on the field.

You can do the same thing in your garden on a smaller scale, if necessary. You might find it easier, though, to shape raised beds for your garden rows, with ditches between. At least that way excess water stands in the ditches and not on your rows of vegetables.

Other Solutions

Where you can get no outlet for a tile drain, and are bothered by just a spot or two of low-lying ground, you can alleviate the condition somewhat by digging a hole with a post-hole digger down about six feet and filling with gravel, again up to a foot from the surface. Water won't stand as long on the surface anyway. Sometimes a hole like that can be punched down through the rock or clay layer that was keeping the water from percolating, in which case you will achieve a fairly effective drain. I once had a garden where the soil was thin and drained poorly due to a layer of bedrock only two feet below the surface. A sewer line was installed on the property next to the garden which entailed a very deep ditch down through the rock. Though fifty feet away, the ditch effectively drained my garden because the water in the entire area had a way to escape deep into the ground.

If you have a real problem wet hole, don't fight it. Make a small pond, a cranberry bog, or a bit of frog swamp out of it. Every piece of property should have a bit of swamp anyway. If every square foot of ground in this country is drained—as some people seem to want to do—then we'd lose our natural water storage areas. From swamps, ponds, and low wet seepy woodland areas, oozes water to tide plants over summer drought. If we tile the whole nation so that all excess water is removed within forty-eight hours after it falls from the sky, we will certainly be encouraging the drying-up of our ground water sources.

Irrigation

In semiarid climates, irrigation is necessary for gardening. The danger, which becomes clearer each day, is that we are using irrigation water too much—wasting it both in the manner in which it is applied and the crops to which it is applied. A great portion of the water applied to the land in giant sprinklers evaporates before it can do the plants any good. It seems to me that the stubbornness which compels ranchers in places like the Nebraska sandhills to try to raise irrigated corn is slightly stupid. They might at least grow grain sorghum,

AVERAGE PRECIPITATION MAP

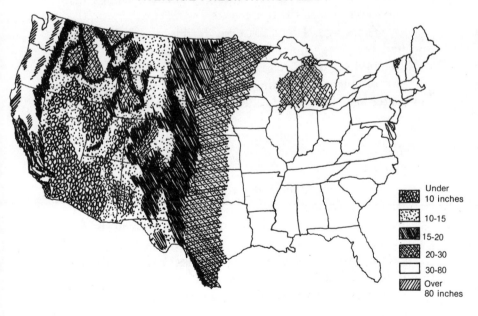

	Under 10 inches
	10-15
	15-20
	20-30
	30-80
	Over 80 inches

which requires less water and makes better yields than corn under Plains conditions. But Nebraska believes it has "unlimited" water under its land, just as the early pioneer in Pennsylvania thought he had "unlimited" lumber.

Anyway, new ideas in irrigation are being tried, and some of them are certainly applicable to gardens. Drip or trickle irrigation will give excellent results, especially in conjunction with mulch, while using only minimal amounts of water. Drip irrigation means applying water through hose systems directly to the plant—even to the plant roots—in small quantities, at more or less frequent intervals, rather than steadily all day or night long. For instance, at the Ohio Research Center, Wooster, Ohio, scientists found they could boost growth on dwarf apple trees with a one hour a day application of two gallons of water per tree. Hoses carry the water from a two-inch main to the trees, where small rubber tubes (called emitters) with very small openings drip the water next to the tree trunks.

Years ago, I bought some flexible plastic hose that had very small holes in it, designed for drip, or maybe I should say ooze irrigation, unrolled the hose along the row of plants according to directions, and turned the water on. Moisture welled from the holes slowly and most of it sank into the soil rather than evaporating into the air. I piled mulch on top of the oozing hose, and a three hour application was enough that way to last a week.

On lawns and on larger acreages in general, sprinkler irrigation is more practical than drip. You will conserve water and help your soil and plants more if you sprinkle at night.

In arid and semiarid regions like California where irrigation ditches have been installed for years, ditch irrigation may be handy to your garden. If so you're in luck.

The system applies the water exactly where it is needed, and in amounts both the soil and the plant can handle most efficiently.

e heart of the drip irrigation system.

Watering the garden in the traditional mode. But a lot of the water never does the plants any good in the traditional mode. Soaker hoses are similar to the sprinkler hose pictured, yet are more efficient in using water.

COMMERCIAL SUPPLIERS OF DRIP IRRIGATION SYSTEMS

Submatic
P.O. Box 246
Lubbock, TX 79406

Drip Irrigation Corp. of America
16140 Raymer St.
Van Nuys, CA 91406

Balm Grove Service, Inc.
Balm, FL 33503

Chapin Watermatics, Inc.
Box 298
Watertown, NY 13601

Drip-Eze Inc.
Box 953
El Cajon, CA 92022

General Irrigation Co.
Box 588
Carthage, MO 64836

Rinko Irrigation Systems, Inc.
395 Smith Street
Brooklyn, NY 11231

Incline Plant Products
Incline Village, NV 89450

Salco Irrigation Systems
3772 Selby Avenue
Los Angeles, CA 90034

Spot Heaters, Inc.
Box 278
Sunnyside, WA 98944

Subterrain Irrigation Co.
1740 So. Zeyn Street
Anaheim, CA 92802

Uni-Flow Corp.
Box 772
Northridge, CA 91324

Water Master Aqua Data Co.
Box 3007
Arcadia, CA 91006

Water Saver Systems
Box 2037
Pomona, CA 91767

Erosion Control

Maybe you have deep, well-drained soil and plenty of rainfall. Then your problem with water is how to control it so you don't lose the soil or what you put on your land. In this respect, protection of soil becomes more than just making your vegetable garden grow. Your house rests on soil. So do your driveway and lawns. Where the limitations of the soil and the effect of rainfall have not been adequately understood, houses have ridden down hills on mud slides, driveways have been covered with silt, and lawns have been sluiced into gullies. Erosion is a problem on a small suburban lot as well as on a large farm.

Erosion problems can creep up on you in unsuspecting ways. Here's an example—an experience that happened to me, in my yard, in front of my eyes. Even though trained to spot potential erosion problems, I did not catch this one until it became critical.

Our lot of approximately two acres sat on a gentle, almost level slope nearly 700 feet from one end to the other. Water can gain quite a bit of momentum in that length, even if the grade is very slight.

At the lower end of the property grew an ash tree around which was a deep, luxuriant sod. As the tree grew larger and denser each year, shading the ground under it more all the time, the grass became thinner.

Many people believe soil erosion was a problem of the dust bowl era that was licked by proper conservation techniques. Although soil erosion, which causes gullies like these, can be licked, *failure* to practice conservation has allowed eroded soil to remain America's worst pollutant.

It was a very gradual process, not something that seemed to demand instant attention. Five years elapsed. Then came the year of the great rains, as we referred to it. As it happened, the natural flow of run-off water from our lot passed under this ash tree, but as long as the area had been heavily sodded, that fact was hardly observable. After heavy downpours, the rain water raced over the nearly bare ground under the tree, and one morning I awoke to see a gully being formed in my yard.

It got worse before I could get rid of the ugly thing, although the cure was simple. All I had to do was cut the lower limbs of the tree off so sunlight could again reach the ground around the tree. Then I smoothed out the soil, reseeded with a grass that liked partial shade, sprinkled chopped straw over the ground for mulch, and laid some old chicken wire fence on top of the mulch to hold it from washing away. But it took two years to gully-proof that lawn again.

Storm Runoff

Erosion is an ever-present danger in many other ways, which may elude you at first. Water was never meant by nature to be collected on roof tops and funneled through gutter downspouts. As it shoots out the lower end, water is turned into a lethal weapon to plants and soil. Not properly contained, that stream of water can cut a flower bed to ribbons or gouge out a ditch in your lawn.

Water cannot soak into street pavement and parking lots. It gathers and begins to roll downhill. At the bottom of hillside streets, I've seen that water actually cut under and lift three-inch layers of blacktop as if they were pages in a book.

Those who have lived in an area before and after it was "developed" with houses, shopping centers, etc., understand how readily a concentration of rooftops and pavement increases flooding. Where previously a four-inch downpour would soak mostly into the ground, now *flash* floods are common. I've seen tiny creeks after twenty years of peaceful coexistence with man suddenly develop into raging torrents capable of floating Volkswagens out of parking lots. The first time that happened everyone laughed. The second time, a car contained a passenger. She panicked, jumped out of the car, and drowned . . . in a body of water that for centuries had rarely been more than a tiny rivulet.

On the other hand, a properly designed suburb can protect soil from erosion far better than can agriculture. Next time you get a hard rain at your place, jump in the car and drive out to nearby farming country. Run-off water gushing down ditches there will invariably be brown with eroding topsoil. Now drive to an established suburb. Often water running off the lawns, golf courses, parks, wooded areas, and streets is bluish-green in color indicating it carries little or no silt.

·Conservation in agriculture can save much soil, but tilling large areas of land leaves the soil vulnerable in a way that can never be completely protected. The suburbs, if people would only restructure their values, can become a Shangri-La for a protected natural environment.

Soil Conservation at the Homeplace

A new house is most vulnerable to erosion, surrounded as it is by bare soil left from construction—and often not good soil at that. As quickly as possible, get that soil covered with some kind of vegetation. Your own interests, apart from a concern for the environment, are at stake. One heavy downpour could deposit most of that soil on your driveway (or worse, your neighbor's driveway). Sodding is, of course, the best way to get quick protection, but many of us can't afford that much sod. It might pay anyway to sod embankments at least—

any place where a steep grade could turn into a gully overnight.

Lacking sod, seed down all the bare soil as quickly as you get it in shape. Any good lawn mixture will do. Put lime down too. I would certainly mix in some rye grass, which comes up quickly, if it is not in the mixture. Rye is not a good permanent lawn grass, but in the beginning you ain't particular. Even weeds are better than nothing. If you can cover the seeded lawn with a light mulch, so much the better. Chopped hay or straw works fine.

Steep banks, too hard to mow easily, eventually can be established in permanent ground covers like pachysandra, vinca, or English ivy. Rooted cuttings from these plants, or sections with roots from established plantings, can be set about a foot apart both ways, even where you have also planted grass seed. Eventually the ground cover will take over and you will only have to do a little hand weeding until it becomes thick enough to shade out most other growth. It's better than risking life and limb trying to manhandle a mower on a steep bank.

Soil conservation practices designed originally for farm land can be tailored to small homestead gardens. Whenever possible, cultivate your garden with cross-slope rows, not up-and-down-hill rows. Such rows can be laid out to follow the contour of the slope, but on small lots, you don't have to go to that much trouble. Straight across rows are okay, but never down the slope.

Grass beds between strips of garden make an attractive landscape and reduce erosion potential. If your lot is quite steep, terraces will make gardening possible without erosion.

If run-off from sloping land above your property causes a problem, you can solve it with a diversion and lessen damage by making it run over a grass waterway through your property. A diversion is a very low, small ridge, usually about a foot high, that follows the contour of the slope and, like a little dam, stops water running downhill, forcing it to follow the diversion ridge to a grass waterway, a ditch, or other safe outlet. The diversion should be kept in sod, its sides low and sloping enough to be mowed. Usually, a little channel ditch on

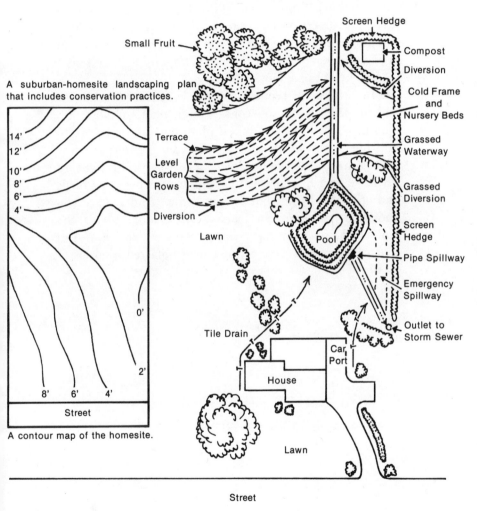

A suburban-homesite landscaping plan that includes conservation practices.

A contour map of the homesite.

117

the up-hill side of the diversion is maintained to guide the run-off water along.

A grass waterway is a wide-bottomed, shallow ditch on a grade that will carry run-off water over it slowly enough so that a dense sod on the waterway will not be eroded. You will see waterways on gentle hillsides of cultivated fields on well-managed farms. A grass waterway or a diversion needs to be designed properly by a competent engineer. Your local soil conservation agent is at your service. Call him. That's why we pay him a salary out of tax money.

In fact, upon request, your soil conservation agent will prepare you a soil conservation plan for your lot. You may not need a detailed plan, but it won't hurt to talk over your ideas with a competent conservationist. If you have a large lot, perhaps you would want to preserve part of it naturally—a place for bees and birds and other wild things to feel at home. And a place you and your children can learn a little more about the biological life chain that keeps us from extinction. (And a place you won't have to mow every blasted week!)

Chapter 8

Soil Acidity and Alkalinity: When To Lime and When Not To

With your moisture problems solved or at least with the solutions underway, your next important step to a good, healthy soil is developing and maintaining the right balance between acidity and alkalinity for the plants you want to grow. Your soil can get acid stomach too.

Though a few plants, like blueberries, flourish in fairly acid soil, most garden crops, lawn grasses, trees, and shrubs like only a slightly acid soil or a neutral soil. Moreover, microorganisms and chemical elements in the soil work more vigorously to make nutrients available to plants when the soil is nearly neutral rather than too acid or alkaline.

Measuring Soil Reaction

Acidity and alkalinity are measured in pH units, the "pH" being a sort of formulaic symbol referring to

119

relative measurements on a logarithmic scale. The letters refer to potential hydrogen, and indicate the breakdown or ionization of water into the hydrogen ion (a positively charged atom), and an oxygen-hydrogen ion (a negative charged molecule unit consisting of one hydrogen and one oxygen atom). Since water is a very stable compound, only a very little of this ionization actually takes place.

Nevertheless, soil alkalinity or acidity is determined by this breakdown. It is caused by the reaction of various mineral and organic compounds with moisture in the soil.

On a pH scale from 1 to 14, 1 is extremely acid and 10 or more extremely alkaline. A peat bog can have a pH as low as 3; an arid desert alkaline soil, as high as 10 or 11.

A pH of 7 is neutral. Every unit of difference in pH represents ten times more acidity or alkalinity. For example, a soil with a pH of 5.5 is ten times more acid than a soil with pH of 6.5. A pH of 8.5 is ten times more alkaline than 7.5. But the difference proceeds logarithmically—a pH of 4.5 is *one hundred* times more acid than a pH of 6.5. That's why it is much easier to lower pH artificially with acid material from 6.5 to 6, but quite difficult to take it from 6.5 down to 4.5. Most plants tolerate well only a fairly small pH range—from 6 to 7. A few will grow at a pH of 4; above 8, I don't know of any plant that will grow well, if at all.

Garden books list plants according to their pH preference, but I'm not so sure this can be done with any exactitude unless all soils the world over were the same —which is far from being true. Some plants will respond a bit differently to pH in different soils. Other plants tolerate a comparatively wide pH range—corn, wheat, and strawberries will, in some cases, do okay in a pH of 5, 6, or 7.

In general, the acid-loving plants thrive with pH around 4.5: blueberry, cranberry, azalea, laurel, rhodo-

Soil pH Conditions and Plant Environment	pH	Verbal Designations of Soil Acidity/ Alkalinity	Familiar Products With Acidity/ Alkalinity Indicated
	0		
	1		Hydrochloric acid
			Phorphoric acid
	2		Lemons
			Vinegar Grapefruit Apples
	3		Good grass silage Super phosphate
Found rarely in organic soil surface layers			Tomatoes Beer
Found occasionally in some soils in humid regions	4		
Suitable for blueberries, azaleas, and rhododendrons		Very strongly acid	Poor grass silage
Typical of many unlimed soils of humid regions—suitable for potatoes	5	Strongly acid	Boric acid Fresh beans
Suitable for grasses but 6.5 would be better		Medium acid	Distilled water open to air
Suitable for gardens, commercial vegetables and grasses	6	Slightly acid	Fresh corn
Best for growth of most forage crops		Very slightly acid	Cow's milk
Suitable for alfalfa but not necessary; danger of overliming injury on sandy soils	7	Neutral, very slightly alkaline	Distilled water in absence of air Human blood
Hazard of deficiencies of boron and manganese		Slightly alkaline	Manure
Ground limestone has a pH of 8.3 A pH above 8.3 is caused by sodium	8	Medium alkaline	Sea water
Found only in alkaline soils of arid west or where materials such as wood ashes have been used in excess		Strongly alkaline	Bicarbonate of soda
	9	Very strongly alkaline	
	10		Milk of magnesia
	11		Ammonia
			Washing soda
	12		Trisodium Phosphate
	13		Lye
	14		

dendron, most broad-leaved evergreens. Between 5.5 and 6.5, put watermelon, sweet potatoes, wild flowers, blackberries, dewberries, black raspberries, wild and some tame strawberries, turnips, cedars, dogwoods, and most plants that you find growing in woodsy, swampy areas. Most other vegetables, fruits, grasses, grains, and trees like a pH of about 6.5. Alfalfa, clovers, bluegrass, and asparagus seem to do best with a pH right at 7.

SUITABLE pH RANGES FOR VARIOUS CROPS AND ORNAMENTAL PLANTS

Crops	pH Range (approx.)
Alfalfa	6.2–7.5
Alsike Clover	5.5–7.5
Apples	5.5–7.0
Asparagus	6.0–7.5
Azalea	4.5–5.5
Barley	6.0–7.5
Beans, Lima	5.5–6.8
Beans, Snap	5.5–7.0
Beans, Velvet	5.5–6.5
Blueberries	5.0–6.0
Buckwheat	5.5–7.0
Cabbage	5.5–7.5
Carrots	5.5–7.0
Corn	5.5–7.5
Cotton	5.5–7.0
Cowpeas	5.5–7.0
Crimson Clover	5.5–7.0
Cucumber	5.5–7.0
Grasses, many kinds	5.5–7.5
Hydrangea, Blue Flowered	4.5–5.5
Iris, Blueflag	5.0–7.5
Juniper, Irish	5.0–6.5
Kale	5.5–7.5
Lettuce	6.0–7.0
Mustard	6.0–7.5
Oats	5.0–7.5
Onions	6.0–7.0
Parsnips	5.5–7.0
Peas	6.0–7.5
Peppers	5.5–7.0
Pine, Longleaf	4.5–5.5
Pine, Yellow	5.0–6.0
Potatoes, Sweet	5.0–6.0
Potatoes, White	4.8–6.5
Radishes	6.0–7.0
Red Clover	6.0–7.5
Rye	5.0–7.0
Sorghum	5.5–7.5
Soybeans	6.0–7.0
Spinach	6.0–7.5
Squash	6.0–7.5
Strawberries	5.0–6.5
Sudangrass	6.0–7.5
Sweetclover	6.5–7.5
Timothy	5.5–7.0
Tobacco	5.5–6.5
Tomatoes	5.5–7.0
Trefoil, Birdsfoot	5.0–7.0
Vetch	5.5–7.0
Wheat	5.5–7.5
Whiteclover	5.5–7.0

Soil Acidification

Cultivated soil in humid regions will become increasingly acid if steps are not taken to reverse the process. That's because soil water will dissolve the more alkaline substances like calcium, sodium, magnesium, and potassium faster than acidic materials like carbon. In soil management language, the alkalis "leach out" sooner than the acids.

Why plants won't tolerate highly acid conditions is not completely understood. Slowdown of beneficial microorganismic action is part of the reason; increased toxicity from certain trace elements like aluminum is another. Deficiency of calcium and magnesium is a third possibility. The best explanation may be that in acid soils, chemical reaction can lock up major nutrients, especially phosphorus, making them unavailable to plants.

Heavy use of inorganic, high-analysis fertilizers is known to cause soil to become more acid. Organic gardeners don't have to worry about that, but the same result can stem from using organic fertilizers that have an acidifying effect. Cottonseed meal is a prime example. Mixing a little bone meal with it helps head off the problem.

Determining Your Soil's pH

The surest way to determine the pH of your soil is to have a good soil test done, which we've already talked about. A simple test for pH you can do yourself is with blue litmus paper, available from drug stores. Blue litmus turns pink when brought into contact with an acid (even a weak acid like vinegar) and turns back to blue if dipped in limewater. Okay. Get some soil from the garden. Try to take soil under the surface

123

rather than off the top. Get samples from two or three different locations. Mix up all the soil you've collected in a clean bucket, then pour clean rain water over it. Place several pieces of litmus paper into the mud you've made in the bucket, being careful that your hands are clean of any acid substance before you handle the paper. Wait ten seconds or so and withdraw one piece of the paper. Rinse it off with clean rainwater. If pinkness shows already, the soil is quite acid. The intensity of the pink color is another indication of degree of acidity.

Pull another piece of the paper out in about five minutes. If pink, the soil needs lime, but not as much as when the color changes right away. If after fifteen minutes the blue paper shows little or no change to pink, your soil probably doesn't need lime.

This method is none too exact. But it will give you an idea of where your soil stands.

Curing Acid Soil

Lime is the cheapest and easiest way to cure acid soil disorders. Freshly burned lime is called quicklime; hydrated lime has been slaked. Don't use quicklime, because it can destroy soil humus. Hydrated lime might too, but it or ground limestone are the preferred materials. Hydrated lime is more potent than ground limestone and acts quicker. Where you would apply fifty pounds of ground limestone to a 1,000-square-foot plot, thirty-five pounds of hydrated lime would be sufficient.

Agricultural-ground limestone is the commonest and safest liming material in use. There are two kinds, generally: calcic limestone and dolomitic limestone. I prefer the latter because it contains magnesium in addition to calcium and so fertilizes a little better while it neutralizes the soil.

A general rule of thumb in applying limestone is this: to increase pH by one unit, spread on every 1,000 square feet thirty pounds of limestone, if the soil is very sandy; if a sandy loam, spread fifty pounds; on a loam, seventy pounds; and on a heavy clay, eighty pounds.

Spread the lime on top of the soil in the fall *after* you have plowed, rototilled or spaded deeply. Lime should not be plowed under, because it leaches down into the soil too fast anyway. On lawns and pastures, spread in late summer if possible, though any time will do. It's best not to apply lime with other fertilizers. And don't use hydrated lime where plants are already growing in the garden. Hydrated lime can injure plant roots. Furthermore, don't lime areas around your acid-loving plants, nor any area where run-off water might carry the lime downhill to such plants. Lime is poison to blueberries, azaleas, and the like.

I believe that the very best way to lime soil is with unleached hardwood ashes. You can't get them in quantity or if you could, they'd be too expensive, but use them whenever you can. If you have a fireplace or are heating and cooking with a wood stove, save the ashes as if they were gold. If you can't put them directly on the soil, store in a dry place, since rain quickly leaches out the lime and potash in them.

I know that the hardwood ashes give me a better liming effect than lime, but I can't prove it. Some of the old agricultural writers, writing at a time when wood ashes were easier to get, observe the same thing. Part of the better response I get from wood ashes on sweet corn is due to the potash in the ashes, but I think the lime must also be in a more available form, too, than in limestone.

Coal ashes are of little or no value.

When using ground limestone, don't expect a tremendous response the first year you apply it. The year after will be better. About every four years liming will usually need to be repeated.

However, where it is really needed, liming gives

fantastic results. Because of that, the temptation is to over-lime, a mistake easy to make on a small garden plot. Over-liming is as bad as not liming at all. A pH of 7.5 is a signal you've overdone it.

Curing Alkaline Soil

A slight alkalinity can be cured sometimes with a little borax and manganese, but be guided at all times by soil tests when using these trace mineral elements. It doesn't take much boron to kill a plant.

Farmers in semiarid regions often use gypsum, which is calcium sulphate, to add calcium to soil that is already alkaline enough—or too alkaline. A great deal of controversy rages around the merits of gypsum or the lack thereof. Chemical farmers don't agree on its efficacy and organic farmers don't agree on whether organically certified producers ought to use it.

If you believe sulfur is a legitimate, natural product for organicists, it is certainly one of the easiest ways to increase acidity. Two pounds per 100 square feet will lower pH about one unit.

A better way to acidify soil is with naturally acid organic materials—acid muck from swamps, oak leaves, oak sawdust, or ground up oak bark, cottonseed meal or acid peat moss.

Ultimately, experience can tell you pretty well when lime is needed. Indeed, some gardeners never test their soil. They depend, instead, on native weed and shrub growth to indicate what the soil needs. This sometimes works but is rather risky, since weed roots often go to greater depths than those of crop plants, reaching a soil of different pH than that near the surface.

In general, however, the natural pH of a large area can often be determined by natural plant growth there, even though plots within that area can be quite different.

Some helps are:

- Hard water in area springs and wells usually indicates abundant calcium carbonate (lime) in the soil, and, therefore, an alkaline condition.
- Native trees of hemlock, white pine, red spruce, oak, and black spruce in relatively large numbers usually means the soil is fairly acid.
- Native trees of American arborvitae (Eastern white cedar) and white spruce in quantity are usually an indication of alkalinity, especially in the subsoil.
- Wild blueberries, most ferns, wild orchids, rhododendrons, and bayberries are all signs of acidity at crop-growing depths.

Or, just watch the clover. If it germinates well and grows healthily, your soil hardly needs lime. When you plant a green manure crop of clover on one of your garden plots (which you should do anyway) lime half of the plot the year before, and not at all on the other. If the limed half grows better, you know what you need to do to the rest of the garden.

Chapter 9

Mulching to Improve Soil

The same cure rarely solves two different problems, but mulching is a kind of minor miracle. It can cure a dozen garden problems, some of them directly related to soil improvement.

- Mulching improves the ability of dry, sandy soils to retain moisture and nutrients.
- Mulching mellows tough clay soils.
- Mulching keeps any kind of soil moist during dry spells and controls erosion and crusting of the soil surface during wet weather.
- Mulching adds fertility to the soil that would cost you a lot of money if you tried to buy it in a sack.
- Mulching moderates soil temperature—warmer in winter and cooler in summer.

Before applying these benefits to solving specific

problems, study how nature uses mulch to improve soil. In woodland country, the leaves fall to earth each autumn, layer upon layer. The bottom layer is constantly rotting and being absorbed as humus into the soil through the action of water, air, worms, insects, and microorganisms. The fertility causes the trees to grow much better, which in turn put out much more of a leaf crop. More leaves result in much more mulch turning into humus and so on, in nature's ever-increasing crescendo of fertility. In a drier grassland region, the grass performs the same job the leaves take care of in a more humid region. The grasses fall over at the end of the growing season, and rot away year after year, building

The year-'round mulch has been popularized as a no-work technique for gardening. The many positive benefits of a thick blanket of organic material, such as this straw, make mulching a practical gardening technique, even for gardeners who like to putter around their vegetables and fruits.

up a deep topsoil. When you pile leaves around your berry bushes as a permanent mulch year after year, or when you mow green manure crops and let them lie on the ground to rot, you imitate nature to the letter.

Mulch As Soil Conditioner

If you garden on sandy soils, mulching can be a most helpful and practical tool for soil improvement. You can, as organic gardeners have demonstrated, keep a sandy vegetable garden under a permanent mulch, dispensing with cultivation altogether. Just pull the mulch back in spring, make a planting trench with a hoe, and sow the seed, replacing the mulch when the seedlings are tall enough.

As the mulch rots into humus, the latter firms up the sandy soil, making it more absorbent. With such porous soils, you need not even turn the mulch under. The humus will work down by itself. Only when weeds and grasses become a problem (which they will after several years of permanent mulch) do you need to plow and remulch. Growing a green manure crop before going back to vegetables will further improve the sandiness.

Sandy gardens are the rule along seasides. Maybe that's why nature put two mulching materials so close at hand—salt hay and seaweed. Salt hay is a clean mulch with very little weed seed in it, while seaweed is rich in trace elements often lacking in sandy soils. Neither will increase acidity—a problem on most sandy soils.

Loosening Clay and Adobe Soils

On tough clay and adobe soils, your problem—improving tilth, aeration, and drainage—is different, but the cure is the same: mulch. But you can rarely keep a permanent mulch on problem clay soils, at least not until you have mellowed them considerably. You almost

130

have to cultivate heavy soils each year in order to get a seed bed fine enough for good germination. To cultivate in the spring, the soil must warm up and dry out properly. That means removing the mulch from early spring until June or whenever hot weather arrives in your area.

Assuming that you have drained, limed, and perhaps green manured a tough clay plot, managed mulching will eventually turn hard clay to crumbly loam. As long as the mulch is organic, it doesn't matter what material you use, but the coarser ones will loosen the clay faster: chopped corn stalks, chopped sugar cane stalks (bagasse), peat moss, shredded bark, wood chips, hay and straw. On tough soil apply a layer of peat moss about three inches deep. That means a bale will cover approximately thirty-eight square feet. A two-inch covering will stretch a bale to treat fifty-six square feet. A bale of bagasse or corn fodder is roughly equivalent. A proper straw mulch deep enough to control weeds and prevent alternate freezing and thawing in winter takes about one standard two-string straw bale for every 200 square feet. The same with hay.

Some gardeners advocate mixing sand into tough clay soils to hurry the mellowing process. Theoretically, that works fine; in practice, you need a lot more sand than you might imagine and the mixture is not always satisfactory. If you are going to the trouble and expense of hauling sand in quantity, you might as well buy good topsoil instead.

Working Mulch into the Soil

Don't bury your mulch under the soil when you plow. Organic matter completely turned six inches under hard clays will rot slowly. Moreover, if the layer of organic matter is heavy, it can block transpiration of moisture from subsoil to topsoil and back.

A rotary tiller or disk works the mulch into the soil

better than a plow. If you use a plow, adjust it so that when the furrow is turned, a little mulch sticks out of the top of the furrow. In spading ground, keep the mulch sandwiched *vertically between* spadefuls of soil rather than burying it at the bottom of the spading ditch. That way, you actually have "columns" of decaying mulch from the bottom of the trench to the soil surface. Aeration and moisture transpiration are greatly enhanced and the mulch will break down faster.

Making Topsoil of Subsoil

The worst tough clay problem is trying to make topsoil out of subsoil. That's what you have to do often when you move into a new home. Not only may the soil around the house be leather-like subsoil, but the builder may have buried stones, broken bricks, cement blocks, chunks of wallboard, and glops of cement under the surface. On top of that, excessive amounts of lime may have been spilled (a little is generally good), making the soil alkaline.

You won't remedy the situation by dumping a couple of inches of topsoil on top, though that would certainly help. You'll have to remove debris if it's close to the surface of the soil. If buried deeply, the junk won't bother much. If alkalinity is high, spread a couple of inches of acid peat moss or oak sawdust on the soil. After a rain has moistened the soil and the surface is drying but is still somewhat soft, rotary-till the peat into the soil a little.

Next spread three inches of well-rotted manure on the ground and work it in as you did the peat. If alkalinity is not a problem (most subsoils are acid not alkaline) skip the peat treatment, use a little more manure and sprinkle limestone on top of it, before working into the soil.

(*Sow Green Manures*) If the area is to be lawn, have sod put down if you can afford it. If not, sow white clover and bluegrass and pray a lot. Sprinkle a chopped straw or hay mulch or grass clippings about an inch thick over the surface. If the area is not level, lay some chicken wire fencing over the mulch and pin the mesh to the ground with pieces of U-shaped wire. The fencing will keep the mulch from washing away in the event of hard rain. Bird's-foot trefoil is another legume that I have discovered will grow on a subsoil if mulched with straw.

Where you want to make garden rather than lawn, sow rye instead of lawn grasses in the fall, and plow under the next spring. Then plant soybeans and plow them under in July and follow with buckwheat. Plow the buckwheat under (or mow with a rotary mower that chops the vegetation, and then rotary-till). Plant rye in the fall again, plow that under in spring and make garden. Use all the mulch you can around the plants after they come up.

(*Another Solution*) There's another way. Remember, that very tough clay soil is not always tough. After wet weather, when the clay is drying out, there is always a time (often brief) when the clods are at a certain soft stage between wet and dry and will crumble fairly easily. A day later they may be hard as rocks again, but if you catch them right, you can work up a fine seedbed. This is particularly true in spring after winter frosts have mellowed the clay. If in the fall you can disk, plow, or rotary-till hard clay at all (even if only into a rough, cloddy surface) and leave it exposed to winter freezes, it will crumble nicely in spring when it reaches the proper stage of semidryness. When the soil is drying, test it every day. If a small clod will break up easily in your hand with the pressure of your fingers, but is dry enough not to smear mud in your fist, get the tiller out immediately and work the surface into a seedbed. Broadcast oats and alfalfa on the surface at the rate of about eighteen pounds of alfalfa and thirty pounds of

133

oats to the acre. That's very thin for oats, but you want only a catch of it—the alfalfa for green manure is what's important. If you can't figure the seeding rate, just be sure when you scatter the seed that every three square inches of surface area has an average of two oat grains and five clover seeds. Rake the surface gently so the seeds are covered. Mulch as described above if you can. The oats will come up fast, however, and hold the soil fairly well unless the surface is quite steep.

Just before the oats develop seed heads, mow them, letting the clippings fall for mulch. The alfalfa seedlings will be much shorter than the oats, only about two to four inches tall. Try to mow the oats without clipping off the alfalfa, though the latter won't be hurt much by clipping. In the middle of August, clip the alfalfa again. Plow under the following May or June and plant your garden. Red clover can be substituted for the alfalfa, or ladino, or bird's-foot trefoil.

(*The Limited Response*) Where your clay, adobe, or subsoil seems more like concrete than soil, you may have to limit your first efforts at building topsoil strictly to the planting row. Some gardeners in exasperation have done just that—making a fall project of digging a trench with pick and shovel (literally) and filling it with alternate layers of compost, mulch, manure, and the recalcitrant clay. Next spring they set plants which they buy or raise in flats directly into the filled trench and cover the whole plot with more mulch. With favorable rains, vegetables will respond to the "trench treatment" and send roots even into the hard clay beyond. The mulch on top helps mellow the soil, too. You get a crop while you are breaking up your "concrete."

You can use this trick on an even more limited scale. Dig holes about a foot deep with a post-hole digger in the hard clay, fill them with compost and manure, then set your plants. The most extreme example I know of, in using this technique, comes from an orchardist along

Lake Erie. He had property that contained a layer of almost solid rock *over* soil—an unusual situation. He blasted holes down through the rock with dynamite, filled the holes with soil, and started a nice orchard.

Mulch as Soil Protector

Besides conditioning the soil as it rots into humus, mulch protects the soil while it lies on the surface. When you put a chopped straw mulch over newly planted lawns as discussed earlier, the straw holds the seeds from washing away, keeps rain from pounding the soil to a hard crust, and holds moisture so the seedling gets a healthy start in life.

Keep those tomatoes—and your other vulnerable fruits and vegetables—out of the dirt, by covering the soil with a beneficial blanket of organic material. The mulch will keep your shoes clean, too, taking the unpleasantness out of post-rain harvests.

Holding Moisture

If I had any doubts about the moisture retention ability of mulch, I lost them as I watched my tomatoes grow in the driest of all summers in our neck of the woods. I had plowed the soil in earliest spring and rotary-tilled it right away so that the finer soil on top acted as a sort of dirt mulch preventing spring soil moisture from evaporating into the air. As soon as I could after that, I mulched the whole area where I wanted to plant tomatoes with six inches of old but still moist cow manure bedding from the barn. On top of that I spread four more inches of rotted straw from some old bales I had on hand. About the middle of May, I set the tomato plants down through the mulch.

We had only one shower from May 1 until August 1. But the soil under that mulch stayed moist until the middle of July and did not really dry out completely until August, when it finally rained again. The tomatoes grew almost as well as ever, and suffered very little blossom-end rot, usually bad in dry years.

The experience made a staunch mulch believer out of me and gave me a sure-fire recipe for Midwest drought protection. First, work the soil surface fine as early in spring as possible, then cover with six to eight inches of rotted bedding. I'm convinced the results equal five inches of irrigation water. Irrigation would have produced tomatoes more watery and less sweet than mine.

Preventing Erosion

Ground corncobs can heal gullies. Where run-off water is digging a ditch down a hillside or through your garden, pack the washed-out area with them. For some reason, ground corncobs won't wash except under severe flooding situations. In the latter case, place a piece of old rolled fence wire (every farm wood lot I know of has rolls of old fencing lying around rusting away) of the right size to fit the gully, and then dump on the cobs through the wire mesh.

Late fall and winter gardens get muddy and make walking a messy affair that gums up your shoes and packs the earth. Mulch between the rows solves both problems. Shredded bark, available from sawmills where bark is peeled from logs, is excellent pathway mulch. Pine needles are even better and more generally available. But almost any kind of mulch will do the trick.

Stabilizing Temperatures

Mulch was probably first introduced into gardening as protection against temperature extremes, particularly from alternate extremes of freezing and thawing during winter. You put straw on strawberries not only to protect the crowns from winterkill in very cold regions, but to keep the ground frozen most of the winter. When the soil freezes, then thaws, then freezes again all winter, the contractions of the soil literally push shallow-rooted plants right out of the ground. The mulch shades the ground; once frozen, earth under mulch tends to stay frozen until spring thaw.

For the same reason, clovers you are growing for green manure should not be cut late in the fall for hay. A mantle of dead clover plants acts as a blanket over the roots. Unprotected, the plants, especially in the first winter when they have not grown deep into the soil, will heave out of the ground.

Plastic mulches won't improve tilth or fertility of your soil and won't add organic matter. They will, however, retain moisture to some extent, and help the soil warm up faster in spring. Black plastic especially will absorb enough heat from the sun to raise soil temperature to the germination point earlier in spring. Some gardeners spread black plastic over a garden plot in the fall. In spring the plastic absorbs heat and shields the plot from excessive rains. At the arrival of the first

137

warm days, the plastic is peeled back and the ground planted. *This practice works well only in very well-drained, lighter soils.* On heavy soils, the ground won't dry out early enough to make the practice worthwhile.

Mulch As Fertilizer

All organic mulches improve soil tilth and micro-organic action in the soil, so your choice of which to use will depend mostly upon availability. If two materials are equally available, the next question should be : which has the greater fertilizing value? Here's a list of the most commonly available mulches and their approximate content of plant food. Depending on how and where these organic materials originally grew and were stored, their content of major and minor elements vary, but the analyses given here can be used to compare one mulch with another.

Green Manures

The most available of all mulches are the ones you grow yourself as green manure. If you clip these crops and let them lay on the garden plot where they are growing, as explained earlier in the chapter, they will rot and add to the garden's fertility. You can cut the grasses and legumes and use them as mulch elsewhere in the garden. Fresh-cut alfalfa, applied as mulch around asparagus plants in one garden I've visited, gave visibly better growth over nearby unmulched asparagus. Alfalfa and red clover contain about 2 percent to 2½ percent nitrogen (N), .5 percent phosphoric acid (P), and 2 percent potash (K). You can remove a ton of alfalfa per year from a quarter acre plot for mulching elsewhere without lessening appreciably its green manuring effect on the ground it is growing in.

Cuttings from green rye straw grown for a green manure crop can be raked up and used for mulch elsewhere. Cut the rye high when it is about twenty-five to thirty inches tall. That still leaves plenty of stubble (and the roots) for plowing under. The stalks and leaves you remove for mulching contain about 1.5 percent N, .5 percent P, and 1 percent K.

Garden Wastes

The chopped stalks and leaves of other garden crops like sweet corn, beans, peas, and cane sorghum make readily available mulches. Corn and sorghum fodder have little fertilizer value, but these two crops can provide more mulch than any other in the garden. Sorghum

Tuck that mulch close to the plants. Pile it on thickly. And make sure it's organic material, not plastic film, which offers no lasting benefits in soil fertility terms.

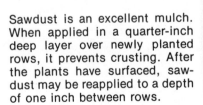

Sawdust is an excellent mulch. When applied in a quarter-inch deep layer over newly planted rows, it prevents crusting. After the plants have surfaced, sawdust may be reapplied to a depth of one inch between rows.

is also one of the better natural sources of sulfur, a necessary trace element.

Pea and bean plants may contain 2 percent N, though soybean hay may analyze as high as 3 percent N and garden beans as low as .25 percent. Pea vines contain about .7 percent K. Be sure to put pea pods back on the garden as they are good sources of P and K. Ashed pea pod wastes from canneries are 27 percent K.

Grass clippings are probably the best mulch in terms of all-around availability. They contain about 1.5 percent N, a smidgen of P, and about 1 percent K. An organicist won't remove all his grass clippings from the

Cocoa bean shells are popular for mulching ornamentals because of their appearance and because they are effective at smothering weeds. Unlike grass clippings or leaves, they are seldom freely available, but they usually are available for the buying at garden centers.

Corncobs, if you can find them, should be especially valued for their moisture holding property. Either whole, as here, or chopped, corncobs make an excellent mulch. Increasingly, corn is being harvested with combines that pick and shell the corn in one operation, shredding everything but the corn kernels and leaving it in the field.

lawn, however, because the soil there can benefit from them, too. But sometimes, especially in June just when you most need mulch in the garden, there are too many grass clippings on the lawn and they have to be raked up anyhow.

Some writer once said in print that grass clippings mat and prevent water from penetrating through to the soil. Since then, many other books have reported that statement. Tain't so, folks. Water will soak through grass clippings quite readily.

Leaves

Tree leaves are best for permanent plantings where root hairs grow close to the surface and would be injured by cultivation. Mounds of leaves over root crops will prevent them from freezing all winter and you can dig as you need. Oak leaves contain .8 percent N, .35 percent P, and .15 percent K, which is about right for most of the common leaves including pine needles. Oak leaves are acid and should be used around acid-loving plants. Maple leaves aren't so acid. White ash leaves are nearly neutral in pH, and are more appropriate to use around vegetables.

Sawdust

Though the fertility value of sawdust is no more than that of leaves, it too is plentiful and often free for the hauling around sawmills. The same for shredded bark.

Straw

Straw and hay by the bale are becoming expensive, but are still the cheapest commercial materials available for mulch in bulk quantities. The straw you buy will almost always be wheat straw, which is about the lowest of all in fertilizing value. It contains an appreciable amount of potash, .8 percent, but millet and buckwheat straw contain over twice that much.

"Old" hay—hay that was ruined or partially ruined by rain before it could be baled and stored under cover— can be purchased reasonably if you can find it. Hay is an excellent mulch for fruit trees, and tests show that mulched apple trees yield better than those in orchards where the soil is cultivated.

Salt hay, the old reliable mulch in the East, contains 1.1 percent N, .25 percent P, and .75 percent K.

Miscellaneous Mulch Materials

Peat, one of the best organic soil conditioners, has little nutrient value. It's usually too expensive to use except on very small gardens.

Buckwheat hulls and cocoa bean hulls are comparatively expensive too, but make a neat, good-looking mulch and are relatively high in nutrient value. Cocoa shells test about 1 percent N, 1.5 percent P, and 1.7 percent K. Buckwheat, as noted above, contains about 2 percent K. Cocoa bean shells are processed with lime

The biggest drawback to newspaper mulch is appearance: it looks awful. Too, newspapers take a long time to decompose, hence are slow to add significantly to the soil. But a heavy layer of newspaper is impenetrable by weeds, making newspapers a boon to gardeners with a particularly tough weed problem.

and should not be put around acid-loving plants. Both of these mulches are quite granular and need to be applied only two inches deep to improve soil tilth.

According to compilations of the USDA, corncob ash is 50 percent K. Perhaps that explains why crops grew so well for many years where we once burned a big pile of cobs.

Seaweed, peanut hulls, spent mushroom compost, and tobacco stems are all good mulches available in specific areas, but unavailable in most other parts of the country. Seaweed can contain 1.5 percent N, .75 percent P, and a healthy 4.9 percent K.

Peanut hulls make a neat mulch when and where they're available, but are not particularly rich in nutrients—.8 percent N, .15 percent P, .5 percent K.

Mushroom compost used to be mostly horse manure. Commercial growers use finely-ground corn fodder, corncobs, straw, and other organic materials. The mixtures are composted and mushrooms grown on them. Afterwards, the used compost is thrown away, or if the demand is high enough, sold at a reasonable price. If you live near a commercial mushroom farm, you can obtain no better mulching material.

Tobacco stems unfortunately are available only in tobacco growing areas as far as I know. They make a satisfactory mulch and are very rich in some nutrients compared to most organic materials. The stems contain nearly 7 percent potash and 2.5 percent or more nitrogen. Because of the nicotine in them, the stems also seem to discourage bugs a little—but not the bugs that feast on green tobacco!

Many other materials available in your area may make good mulch. For instance, around grain elevators you may be able to get chaff and cleanings (called beeswing) by the truck load. The same would be true in the South around cotton ginning operations. The rule is to think mulch all the time and keep your eyes open.

Mulching and Earthworms

A mulched organic garden is always full of earth-worms. In the final analysis that may be the very best soil-improving effect of mulch, because the earthworm is one of the best soil-builders nature provides. The symbol of America ought to be the earthworm, not the eagle, which does very little useful work except eat carrion once in awhile.

Darwin estimated that fifteen tons of dirt per acre passed through earthworm bodies in a year in a fertile soil. He was wrong because he underestimated the aver-age number of worms in an acre. In a really good soil, about twenty-five tons of earthworm castings per acre per year are produced, according to research done in England. Every fifteen years, earthworms can make three inches of new topsoil from castings. Moreover, dirt coming out of the earthworm is ten times richer than it was coming into the earthworm.

Other recent estimates give the earthworm even more prodigious accomplishments. In a good soil, worms can reach a population of 1,750,000 per acre, say some scientists. Each worm can eat dirt equal to its body weight. Fifty worms weigh about a pound. A million worms would move ten tons of dirt a day per acre, ac-cording to this estimate! Such a magnificent tillage feat is accomplished without one speck of labor, fuel cost, or energy use on the part of man.

I was shocked recently in reading the latest edition of one of the leading reference books on gardening, to find that almost every reference to earthworms discussed ways to get rid of them! I can see why an indoor gar-dener would not want worms in his clay pots, but when a homeowner becomes so fussy that he worries about earthworms "tearing the devil out of my lawn," he has a problem all right, but it's not his earthworms. It's his head. Earthworm castings are unsightly only to the ignorant, and if the homeowner wouldn't insist on shaving the lawn down to carpet height with his overpowered lawnmower, he'd never see the castings anyway. Instead, he kills the worms with chlordane, then spends gobs of money and time "thatching" the lawn. Earthworms eat thatch free of charge and also keep the soil under the grass aerated so the grass can thrive.

Even in death, the earthworm contributes to our welfare. At least 1,000 pounds of dead earthworm bodies per acre are decaying in a good organic soil throughout the year. This protein turns back into nitrogen in the process, releasing an estimated forty pounds of available N per acre per year.

You need be neither skillful, learned, nor lucky to get a good worm population in your garden. Just mulch a lot. The worms feed on the underside of the mulch, mixing and combining it with earth in their castings. The more you mulch, the more worms you get. Some soil experts say winter mulch is crucial to earthworms. That may be so in milder climates. In the North, winter mulch is certainly beneficial, but in really cold weather, the worms will burrow deep into the soil and remain inactive anyway. The summer mulch that feeds native worms and keeps the soil moist is more important in the North. But mulch during spring and fall is most important of all because that's when worms are most active.

If you read advertisements for earthworms, you will get the idea that you can buy worms and "seed" them into your garden and get a big population fast. That's not quite correct. Red wigglers do tremendously well in boxes and compost heaps, but they will not always reproduce as well as your own native worms (there are about 2,000 varieties of worms) in the garden.

Just keep mulching, and you'll get all the worms your garden needs.

Chapter 10

The Compost Heap

It is difficult to talk about mulching for a whole chapter without mentioning another of the organic gardener's basic resources—the compost heap. Actually, mulching relies on the same natural process that takes place in a pile of compost—which is why it is often referred to as sheet composting. In both instances, organic matter decomposes and is converted into humus.

Composting is a natural process manipulated by gardeners under closely controlled conditions in the compost heap. All organic matter rots (eventually) in or on the soil. Dead plant roots, leaves on the forest floor, dead animals, all return finally to the humic fold of mother earth. In fact, burying dead bodies in the earth was probably man's earliest use of the wonderful process of composting.

The term compost is a little confusing to gardening beginners. The word is used both for the organic matter

Every garden should have a compost heap next to it
(and vice versa). The heap will consume all the garden
and landscaping wastes, as well as all the kitchen
scraps, turning them into a valuable soil supplement
that boosts soil fertility and tilth.

in the compost heap and for the humus that is produced
in the decomposition process. Technically, one should
say that during the process of composting a pile of organic matter is converted into a humus-like substance, if
not into humus itself.

There are two purposes for the compost heap, both
equally beneficial. First, waste materials are disposed of
in an efficient and sanitary manner. In large-scale mu-
nicipal waste composting, this is the principal purpose.
Second, the compost heap produces a product (humus)
that is one of the best, if not the best, fertilizers and soil
amendments you can use. For a gardener, this second

purpose for building compost heaps is usually the more important, although he is equally aware of the waste disposal advantages of his tidy composting system. Indeed, composting is probably the only "manufacturing" process civilization has yet devised in which neither input nor output is a drain on natural resources. Composting is the one way you can eat your cake and have it too.

Whole books and even a magazine have been devoted exclusively to the subject of composting. (A basic, and somewhat technical, paperback book on the subject is Clarence Goleuke's *Composting: A Study of the Process and Its Principles.* An older and far larger book is *The Complete Book of Composting,* which will tell you everything you wanted to know about composting and then some. The magazine is called *Compost Science.* All are published by Rodale Press.)

Building Your Compost Heap

Of the many ways to approach the compost heap, the one I like is to think of it as a "small livestock" venture, somewhat like a worm ranch or a bee farm. At first glance, that comparison may sound ridiculous, but it can make composting easier to understand for homestead gardeners and farmers like myself.

The compost heap is a big pile of food for the smallest but most necessary "livestock" you are privileged to care for on your land—soil microorganisms. Billions of minute bacteria, fungi, and actinomycetes with voracious appetites eat away in the compost heap, as they do in the soil. Without them there would be no life at all.

In a well-made compost heap so many microorganisms live that numbers are meaningless. Scientists calculate microorganism population at ten to the seventh power in every gram of composting material—and there are 435 grams to the pound! Other estimates go as high

BACTERIA, ACTINOMYCETES, AND FUNGI ISOLATED FROM COMPOST

BACTERIA
Mesophilic
  Cellumonas folia
  Chondrococcus exiguus
  Myxococcus virescens
  M. fulvus
  Thiobacillus thiooxidans
  T. denitrificans
Thermophilic
  Bacillus stearothermophilis

ACTINOMYCETES†
Thermotolerant and Thermophilic
  Micromonospora vulgaris
  Nocardia brasiliensis
  Pseudonocardia thermophila
  Streptomyces rectus
  S. thermofuscus
  S. thermophilus
  S. thermoviolaceus
  S. thermovulgaris
  S. violaceoruber
  Thermoactinomyces vulgaris
  Thermonospora curvata
  T. fusca
  T. glaucus
  Thermopolyspora polyspora

FUNGI
Mesophilic
  Fusarium culmorum
  Stysanus stemonitis
  Coprinus cinereus
  C. megacephalus
  C. lagopus
  Clitopilus pinsitus
  Aspergillus niger
  A. terreus
  Geotrichum candidum
  Rhizopus nigricans
  Trichoderma viride
  T. (lignorum) harzianum
  Oospora variabilis
  Mucor spinescens*
  M. abundans*
  M. variens*
  Cephalosporium acremonium*
  Chaetomium globosum*

Thermotolerant and Thermophilic
  Aspergillus fumigatus
  Humicola insolens
  H. griseus var. thermoideus
  H. lanuginosa (Thermomyces
    lanuginosus)
  Mucor pusillus
  Chaetomium thermophile
  Absidia ramosa
  Talaromyces (Penicillium)
    duponti
  Sporotrichum thermophile
  S. chlorinum
  C.t. 6 (Mycelia sterilia)
  Stilbella thermophila
  Malbranchea pulchella
    var. sulfurea
    (Thermoidium sulfureum)
  Thermoascus aurantiacus
  Byssochlamys sp.
  Torula thermophila

†Treated separately because of their common occurrence in compost.
*Probably mesophilic, but not definite with available data.

as 2,000 times that above-mentioned amount, whatever ten to the seventh power is. Of the *known* kinds of microorganisms in compost, seven are bacteria, fourteen are actinomycetes, and thirty-four are fungi (see table below).

Just as with any successful livestock venture, you must feed your microorganisms a correctly balanced "ration" and make sure their living quarters are well ventilated, properly humidified, and kept at a proper temperature.

A Balanced Ration

Soil microorganisms "eat" mostly carbon and nitrogen—carbon for growth and nitrogen for protein synthesis. They like best a mixture of thirty parts carbon to one part nitrogen. The quantity of carbon as related to the quantity of nitrogen in any kind of organic matter is called the "carbon/nitrogen ratio." Soil scientists like to make this concept sound terribly complicated in keeping with its importance, but a simple understanding of

CARBON/NITROGEN RATIOS OF VARIOUS ORGANIC MATERIALS	
Food wastes (table scraps)	15-1
Sewage sludge: activated	6-1
digested	16-1
Wood	700-1
Sawdust	500-1
Paper	170-1
Grass clippings	19-1
Leaves	a range of 80-1 to 40-1
Fruit wastes	35-1
Rotted manure	20-1
Sugar cane residues	50-1
Cornstalks	60-1
Straw	80-1
Alfalfa hay	12-1
Humus	10-1
Alfalfa	13-1
Green sweetclover	16-1
Mature sweetclover	23-1
Legume-grass hay	25-1
Oat straw	80-1

how to apply c/n ratios to your "feeding operation" will suffice for practical gardeners.

Microorganisms wax healthy on a diet of organic matter with a c/n ratio of 30 to 1 (textbooks usually just say 30. The "to 1" is taken for granted), or more properly within a range of 26 to 1 to 35 to 1. But the c/n ratio varies with the type of organic matter—alfalfa hay can have a c/n ratio as low as 12 to 1, sawdust as high as 500 to 1 (See table). Therefore, you must mix organic materials in your heap so that they approximate the 30 to 1 ideal mixture. If you try to make a compost heap out of fresh sawdust only, it will take a long time to decompose. Add nitrogen to bring the c/n ratio to 30 to 1, and the sawdust will heat up and decompose much more rapidly. Another example: with tree leaves at a 50 to 1 c/n ratio, combining them with green grass clippings at a 20 to 1 c/n ratio with about twice as many leaves as grass clippings would make an approximate average of 30 to 1.

One caution. Compost scientists, like all scientists, like numbers and the assumed exactness that goes with them. But the whole compost field is hampered by the fact that there's always the possibility of wide variation in the chemical makeup of organic matter. Grass clippings may contain over 2 percent nitrogen or they may contain less than 1 percent, depending on how they were fertilized, how fresh they are, and so on. Tree leaves can have a c/n ratio that varies from 40 to 1 to 80 to 1. Use tables of formulation as guides only. Building a successful compost heap is as much art as science, and experience will teach you more than tables of numbers.

At any rate, the general principle always applies: a successful compost heap (microorganism-feeding operation) depends upon a mixture of both carbonaceous material and nitrogenous material. The former comes from "harder" kinds of organic matter—dried leaves, sawdust, straw; the latter from green material like grass clippings, or soft material like garbage, or partially processed sources of nitrogen like sewage sludge, manure, rich soil, or humus itself, which has a c/n ratio of 10 to 1.

If you don't get enough nitrogen in the mix, your compost heap may sit there for a year and scowl back at you rather than decompose in three months like good compost piles should. If, on the other hand, you get too much nitrogen in the mix (if the average c/n ratio falls below 26 to 1), the microorganisms go wild. Excess nitrogen produced is converted into ammonia which seeps out of the pile in gaseous form and dissipates into the atmosphere. In addition to nitrogen loss, the compost may begin to stink—as anyone knows who has piled up lush green grass clippings, or worse, allowed them to heat up in plastic bags.

A knowledge of carbon/nitrogen ratios and their connection to the production of humus in the compost heap affords the gardener with an excellent demonstration of the life of the soil where the same humus-producing process is, or should be, going on all the time. Unfortunately, it is the chemical farmer who needs the lesson most, but he doesn't make compost heaps.

To maintain high yields, the modern farmer applies high and increasingly costly amounts of chemical nitrogen. The microbes in the soil go after that nitrogen like kids after candy. If there's not enough carbonaceous organic matter in the soil (and too often there isn't), the microbes use the humus in the soil to get the necessary carbon they need for heat and energy. In so doing, the microbes release the nitrogen in the humus, which nitrogen, along with the chemical nitrogen already applied, is absorbed by the plants. The applied nitrogen gets the credit for raising yields from, say, seventy-five bushels of corn per acre to 125, when actually the nitrogen released from the humus also helped.

But the essential point is that in the process, the

soil's store of humus is literally burned out unless healthy amounts of organic matter are forthcoming. If not, the plant derives all its nitrogen, or an ever-increasing amount of it, from the commercial application. There is no native, stored, slow-release fertility to fall back on, and in the event of shortages (or extremely high prices) of chemical nitrogen, both crop yields and the farmer's economic health fall sharply. The jolt to an economy and a society geared to the higher yields can be severe— as we are presently witnessing, unfortunately.

Moisture

Moisture and oxygen are necessary in adequate amounts to make microorganisms happy. Proper moisture content of the composting materials should be kept around 50 percent—the material should feel wet but not soggy. Sogginess indicates moisture content of 60 percent or more at which aerobic decomposition ceases, replaced by anaerobic decomposition. Anaerobic decomposition depends on a whole different gang of microbes which require only a little oxygen, if any. Anaerobic decomposition is not desirable in garden composting. It is slower and is accompanied by offensive odors, like that of hydrogen sulfide. High moisture only indirectly causes the change. An overly-wet compost heap mats together, especially if the material has not been shredded, and excludes the proper amount of oxygen that aerobic microorganisms need.

If the compost heap is too dry, little or no decomposition takes place. That's why a properly constructed heap has a depression in the top to catch falling rainwater. In dry weather, or when piling together dry material, gardeners keep a hose handy and sprinkle the pile to keep it at about 50 percent moisture content.

Temperature

With proper c/n ratio and moisture, a compost heap

153

will heat up in a day or two after it is built. The materials on the outside of the heap act as insulation to prevent some heat loss, but in really cold weather it's impractical to keep the heat up in the heap. Extra insulation is necessary by covering the heap with hay, straw, soil, or old sacking, or by constructing the heap in a hole. If the hole is not well-drained, it will usually fill up with water, at least partially, and wreck your aerobic processes. (For the same reason, a heap should be protected from *excessive* winter rains.) It's best to start a compost heap no later than late fall so that its heat cycle is well underway before any near zero weather comes along.

Normally the heap will go through a classic two-stage heat cycle. The first stage peaks at 104° F. (40° C.). Then the pile heats on up to 160° F. under the activity of a different type of microbe that can withstand the higher temperatures. The first heat level is called the mesophilic stage, the second thermophilic. At 160° F., harmful pathogens, if any, and weed seeds are killed, but if the compost heap gets hotter than 160° F., the microorganisms can also be killed. When this happens, the temperature of the heap may drop rather quickly. When microorganism populations again increase, the temperature rises until decomposition is complete.

Ventilation

To keep the heap from getting too hot (more a problem on large heaps than on small ones), turning is necessary. Turning is also helpful in speeding the decomposition process, because organic matter on the outside of the heap is turned inward where the temperature is high. This not only exposes all parts of the heap to equal heat of decomposition, but insures that all weed seeds and harmful pathogens are killed by the heat. The aeration of a heap by turning also insures adequate oxygen for the microorganisms.

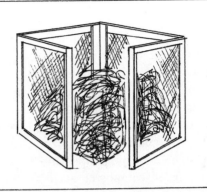

1. Wire and Wood bin: Four panels of wood frame and screening can be latched together to form a movable container that lets air in on all sides. Easy to make and use.

2. Concrete block: It's easy to stack cinder blocks leaving four-inch gaps between them to form a composting bay. Other bays are easily added. Because you use no mortar, you can add and subtract bays and dismantle the structure without trouble.

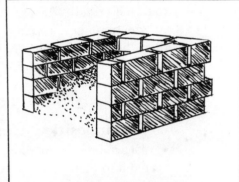

3. Raised pile: This is a great way to let air in from the bottom of the pile. Some folks make compost in a 53-gallon drum set on a platform; both ends removed. Here a wooden frame holds the pile up off the ground for aeration.

4. Buried pit with cover: You can make compost in a pit and use a hatch cover if you live in a crowded neighborhood and you want to avoid any chance of offense, although a properly-made pile doesn't smell or breed flies.

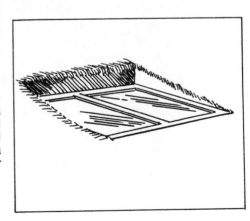

Size

Size of a compost heap depends upon machinery available. Five feet high and five feet wide is probably the maximum size if you are working with hand tools. If you make the compost by hand in bins, you can use smaller sizes. If you are working with power machinery, you can make windrows ten feet wide and at least eight feet tall, but the bigger the heap, the more easily it can overheat, so you will have to plan on turning the windrows more frequently than a garden composter needs to turn his smaller heaps.

Compost heaps need no container structure around them, but containers make a neater operation, help hold heat in, and make rain and winter protection easier. Structures can be made of wood, stone, cement blocks, wire, etc., and vary with the imagination of the gardener.

Decomposition Time

Depending on method, organic matter can be converted into humus in any length of time from two years to two weeks. The shorter the time, the more labor is involved (in turning the compost). The two-week method, which goes by various names, requires several turnings on a strict schedule. The two-year system requires no turning at all. Between these two extremes lies the popular Indore method and its many variations which will make humus in about three months.

To make compost in fourteen days (in some cases, skilled composters have made it in ten days), you must shred the material that goes into the heap. Shredding will facilitate composting in any system, but here it's a necessity. Since the various shreddings are mixed together, layering is unnecessary. The heap is piled five feet high and turned every three days. To speed the decomposition, extra nitrogen is added—manure works fine, but an even richer source, like bloodmeal or cottonseed meal, will give the microorganisms an even faster start. The frequent turning insures that anaerobic decomposition with its unpleasant odor does not replace aerobic action.

The two-year, nonturning method, as practiced by long-time organic gardeners, requires extra space and bins—enough to store two year's production of compost. One Ohio gardener I know keeps about ten bins, measuring four to five feet square and about five feet high, full of compost in various stages of decomposition. He shreds every bit of organic matter that goes into the bins. A bin fills slowly as kitchen scraps become available. Every week or so, the three-gallon can in the kitchen fills with scraps which go into the compost along with five bushels of shredded material (mostly leaves, a bag of grass clippings, a scoop of lime, a scoop of bone meal and seven shovelsful of dirt). After a filled bin has set for a year, the gardener heaps on several shovelsful of finished humus rich in earthworms. The worms multiply quickly in the new environment and help complete the decay process without turning.

The Indore method will produce compost without shredding, but shredding is recommended to insure suc-

LAYERS IN THE COMPOST HEAP

2"-3"		Soil, Wood Ashes, Rock Powders
2"-5"		Manure
12"		Garbage Weeds and Garden Trash Leaves Other Green Matter
24"		

Soil Surface

157

1. Bob Hofstetter, who works at the Rodale Experimental Farm, demonstrates the steps in constructing a compost pile. He uses a shredder for thick clumps of matted leaves. Shredding isn't necessary in making compost, but does speed the process and insure higher temperatures when decomposition heats the pile. Matted clumps of materials such as these leaves should be broken down. If you don't have a shredder, lower your rotary lawnmower blade onto a pile of the materials and blow the shredded residue against a wall for easy collection.

2. Using a pitchfork, Bob scratches up the soil where he intends to build the pile; this exposes the bottom of the pile to soil microorganisms and earthworms, and hastens decay.

3. Next, a layer of green matter —in this case, hay and shredded cornstalks—is placed on the bare spot of ground to start the pile. This layer should be a good foot or two thick and bigger around than you would think, since this is to be the base of the pile. Eight feet is a minimum diameter of this layer for a pile that's to be five feet high.

4. Bob covers the green matter with about one-fifth as much manure. Pig manure is full of trace minerals; chicken manure really gets the pile going hot; cow manure is excellent but not as biologically active as chicken manure; and horse manure is the least active. What you use will most likely depend on what's available.

5. If you have any kitchen garbage available, put it down on top of the layer of manure—this also helps kindle the bacterial "fire" that will push temperatures in the pile center up to 180 degrees Fahrenheit. Kitchen garbage, composed as it is of wastes from food grown in many places, adds lots of trace elements.

6. Now sprinkle on a couple of shovelfuls of rock powders and any wood ashes (don't use coal ashes) you have. The exact proportions of these aren't too important, but if put on too thickly, the powders will cake. Use rock phosphate, potash rock, greensand, marl, crushed limestone —but avoid slaked lime, super-phosphate, and chemical potassium and nitrogen preparations. The materials you want are ground from rock, not made in a chemical factory. These rock particles are slowly and safely dissolved by the acids released when bacteria work on compost, and made available to plant roots that way.

7. Finish the ingredients for this first course of your layered pile by covering the heap with an inch or so of good soil. The soil contains bacteria, and seeds the pile with microorganisms.

8. Now water the pile thoroughly. If you wait until the pile reaches its final height—perhaps three to five courses—the water will tend to run off the sides and leave the center of the pile dry. A dry compost pile won't "work," as the bacteria needs moisture. So wet each course well.

9. The bacteria also need air, and here Bob is laying down a number of sticks on top of the completed first course. After the pile is built, the sticks can be removed, leaving air channels into the center of the pile, or they can be lifted and shaken, which also helps aerate the pile. This step isn't necessary, but it helps the pile achieve maximum temperatures.

10. Begin to put down the second course, using a foot or two of green matter as the first layer, just as before. You'll probably put on from three to five courses before the pile is high enough. The pile will decompose at any height, but when it reaches four to five feet, there's enough bulk to promote really hot temperatures in the center of the pile. These temperatures mean decomposition is proceeding as rapidly as possible. They also mean weed seeds are being destroyed. A pile that gets really hot will be done in a month, if turned a couple of times. A cold pile may take a year to decompose. Don't forget to water each course thoroughly.

11. Finish the pile with a layer of hay or green matter covered with an inch or two of soil. Here Bob is putting down the hay before shaking on the soil. Water one last time and forget it.

cess. A layer of carbonaceous matter is alternated with a layer of nitrogenous wastes to a height of five feet and a width of five to ten feet. Many compost makers like to lay down a layer of branches first and mound the organic matter on them. Also, stakes may be erected along the center line of the prospective pile. Afterwards the stakes can be pulled out, leaving holes for aeration.

The depth of the alternate layers of carbonaceous and nitrogenous wastes varies with the organic material. About eight inches of leaves alternating with four inches of green grass clippings makes a good composition. A six-inch layer of leaves alternating with a two-inch layer

Some gardeners use—swear by—organic compost activators. They usually come in a powder to be applied to the compost heap as is or mixed in a pail of water. Most tests show them to be of doubtful value.

of manure sprinkled with topsoil and lime is another popular and traditional mix. Just bear in mind that scientific experiments have shown that time will depress the formation of nitrogen in the compost heap.

To speed the decomposition you can inoculate your heap with bacterial activators—several commercial brands are marketed for that purpose. Opinions vary greatly on the merits of activators. In tests I'm familiar with, the addition of activators did not measurably increase microbial action in the compost. If the heap was constructed properly, the microorganisms naturally present increased sufficiently to produce humus. If conditions were not adequate for good natural activity, the addition of more bacteria apparently did not overcome the difficulty.

Finished compost—humus—has a carbon/nitrogen ratio of about 10 to 1. It will contain approximately two parts nitrogen, one part phosphorus, and one part potash, with a pH of about 7 or nearly neutral. Though low in nitrogen, phosphorus, and potash, compared to chemical fertilizers, compost seems to produce tremendous growth response in plants, estimated at about eight times more than its mathematical formula would indicate. One reason for such response is the slow release characteristic, already mentioned. Another is the fact that nitrogen in humus does not readily leach away in periods of high moisture. None is wasted, whereas applications of chemical nitrogen that bring the carbon/nitrogen ratio below 25 to 1 can result in a 50 percent loss of nitrogen. Furthermore, humus is generally well endowed with almost all the known trace elements plants need—and perhaps some we don't yet know are essential.

Using Your Compost

Gardeners rarely can use too much humus from their compost heaps. They never have enough to go around and so are inclined to ration the precious stuff rather than overuse it. Two pounds for every 4½ square feet (ten tons per acre) is an adequate treatment, though one could go twice that high before he'd have to worry about nitrate poisoning. Legume crops, which seem to require less nitrogen, in tests have increased in yield as the application of humus was raised from none to five tons per acre. Beyond that, increased humus applications did not increase yields. But on grasses and grains, leafy vegetables and root crops, the more humus the better, within reason. If you work hard enough at composting to supply your land at a rate of one pound per two square feet, you should get the highest award for distinguished service this country gives. Unfortunately, we tend to give such awards mostly to those who have done an outstanding job of killing other people in wars rather than in helping to sustain life on earth. But maybe some day the world will give the year's best humus producer a Nobel Peace Prize.

The Benefits of Compost

Apart from its fertility value, humus is most beneficial as a soil amendment. You can make topsoil with it where you have only denuded subsoil or hard clay. Apply a three-inch layer of humus, digging it in to a depth of six inches with spading fork or rotary tiller. Repeat three years in a row and you'll accomplish what it takes nature at least 100 years to do.

Specific uses for compost take advantage of both its fertility and tilth-restoring values. Humus seems to produce healthy germination and to invigorate seedling growth, so a liberal application in the planting row is most beneficial. Humus applied liberally around roots of transplants (vegetables, bushes, trees) increases the rate of survival and effects quick growth response after the shock of transplanting.

Mulch gardeners often observe, as I have, how easily seeds from trees root and take hold in rotting mulch. In fact, almost any kind of garden seed, like those from last year's residue of rotted tomatoes or squash, will spring to life no matter how carelessly scattered on rotting mulch. There just has to be some very special life-enhancing property to humus. You see it best when you mix humus into your rooting medium. I know that skilled horticulturists can get excellent rooting percentages with almost pure sand, but amateurs like myself, without misting equipment or special covered rooting boxes, get better results by mixing in some humus.

For cold frame and hotbed soil, compost is beneficial too. Mix two parts fertile loam, one part sand, and one part compost.

A couple of tablespoons of compost in potted plants is a good practice. A "tea" made from steeping compost in water is also a good mild fertilizer for house plants.

Compost benefits fruit trees when it is scattered like fertilizer under them. However, I think this is a poor use of the precious stuff. Around permanent plantings like trees, it is more sensible to mulch and let the mulch break down into humus of its own accord. Save your manufactured humus for special purposes as mentioned above or in the tilled parts of your garden.

But no matter how you use the rich black "gold," humus will bring you better gardening. Every time you assist in turning wastes into more humus, you have the extra satisfaction of knowing you are turning the world into a better place to live.

Chapter 11

Soil Amendments, Conditioners, and Natural Fertilizers

Around 1970, Americans trapped in a fake, hoaxed-up world of their own making discovered the organic philosophy and its emphasis on a more natural approach to life. The idea appealed to them so much they tried to make it part of their prefabricated environment. Natural everything became the national fad. We still see advertisements for everything from "organic" dishware (well, it's made from clay, don't you see) to "natural" toenail polish.

It's not surprising that the natural look should come full circle and end where it started—in agriculture. All of a sudden, it would seem, man discovered that gardening and farming should be "natural." The organicist can't help but react with "where have I heard that before?" He's all for natural farming (or "eco-farming" as the new natural farmers like to call it) but what's new?

The new part of the natural farming rash is the proliferation of soil conditioners, serums, activators, and amendments that have accompanied it. Many of these products are good organic soil aids, but the true value of others is still in dispute. A bag full of "natural" magic can be a bigger waste of your money than a can full of chemicals.

Nevertheless, many soil conditioners and natural fertilizers are just what the organic grower is looking for. Others merit a try—at least, they aren't toxic. I'll probably repeat it before this chapter is over, but my advice is this: if a garden supply salesman is trying to sell you some offbeat fertilizing product, you can always

Yes, even organic gardeners can find fertility in a paper sack and remain true to their organic principles. Rock powders are essential. Other products can be a sound supplement to—but not a substitute for—composting, mulching and green manuring to boost organic matter levels in the garden soil.

try it out on a row or two, or a few plants. If you get results you can see and measure, which are better than adjacent rows where you didn't use the product, try the stuff on a little larger basis. In a year or two you'll know whether the material is worth the price. If it isn't, you will not have hurt your bank account in the meantime.

Usage has sanctified the term "natural fertilizer" for some of these products, but manufacturers are rarely able to call them fertilizers—at least not on the label. Most states won't allow anyone to sell a material as fertilizer unless the analysis of nitrogen, phosphorus, and potash is printed on the label. If the analysis of these three nutrients happens to be 0-0-0 or thereabouts, as often is the case with soil conditioners, authorities won't concede the product is a fertilizer, even though it may be beneficial to the soil in other ways.

For every gardener you can find who will give a testimonial in favor of a product, you can find another who'll denounce it. Neither testimonial nor denunciation means a whole lot. In the first case, the gardener may be trying to sell the stuff to his neighbors, and in the latter case, he may not have used the product correctly but doesn't want to admit it. Remember that when you hunt for soil conditioners. I won't be of much help either. I've included as complete a list of products as I can find at the end of the chapter, and I mention a few products for sake of example, but neither by inclusion nor exclusion do I intend approval or disapproval. If you are already doing a good job of organic farming and gardening, you will approach all natural fertilizers cautiously, asking the question: What can this particular product do for my soil that I have not already done?

For sake of convenience the materials are divided into six categories: bacterial inoculants, rock mineral products, seaweed derivatives, humates, organic amendments, and organic, processed fertilizers. The categories overlap sometimes as most classification schemes do.

Bacterial Inoculants

In the earth under your feet lives a family of bacteria called rhizobia. They're about your most important friends because they're responsible for processing nitrogen into a form plants can use as food.

The strains of rhizobia which process nitrogen most efficiently like to live on the roots of legume plants in little nodules the legumes form for them. Scientists have found that by increasing the number of rhizobia bacteria in the soil, they can increase the amount of nitrogen the bacteria will process. The legume plant and the bacteria

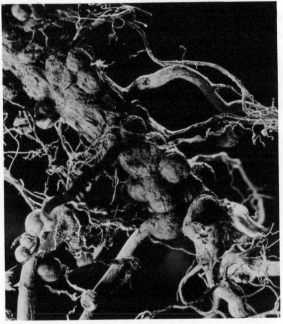

Rhizobia are a form of soil bacteria capable of forming symbiotic nodules on the roots of leguminous plants that help fix nitrogen. The nitrogen spurs the growth of the legume, and, as the nodules reach maturity and disintegrate, fertilizes the soil. A further nitrogen boost can be obtained by leaving the root systems in the soil to rot after the crop is harvested.

169

work together in almost perfect symbiotic relationship. The plant draws in free nitrogen from the air. The bacteria, living in the protection of the root nodules, convert the atmospheric nitrogen into food, enough for the legume plant and other plants around it, with plenty left over if bacteria numbers are high. In scientific terms, the bacteria "fix" the atmospheric nitrogen in the soil where it remains in comparatively stable form until used by growing plants. With modern techniques, these bacteria have a proven capacity of processing nearly 200 pounds of available nitrogen per acre per year. In these times of high fertilizer costs, you can readily see how valuable rhizobia are. If nitrogen from fossil fuels becomes unavailable in sufficient quantity for food production, rhizobia will be priceless.

Agriculturists have been making use of rhizobia's services for decades. Strains of the bacteria, cultured in the laboratory, are applied to the legume seed at planting time. As the seed grows into a plant, the bacteria go to work. In some field tests, inoculating soybean seed has increased yields as much as five bushels per acre. Where soil has been deficient in rhizobia, equally dramatic results have come from inoculating garden pea and bean seed.

Some scientists think legume inoculation can be overdone. They contend that a field which has been regularly inoculated in the past won't need a treatment at every planting. Other agronomists disagree, demonstrating that rhizobia populations tend to decline, especially under intensive row crop cultivation. The higher the rhizobia population is kept, they say, the better the chance of higher yields or higher nitrogen fixation in the soil.

That's about all the reason you need to inoculate your legume seed—especially any clover you grow for green manure—every time you plant. The cost of inoculation is so reasonable and the value of nitrogen produced by the bacteria so high, you can't afford not to. For the organic grower, the practice is doubly rewarding. Seldom do you find a product on the market that requires so little labor to apply and is both inexpensive and easy to handle even on larger acreages. The nitrogen produced, moreover, through the interaction of legume and bacteria, is for you not just a cheaper "alternative" to chemical nitrogen, but quite possibly an *only* source of nitrogen practical for a large garden or field.

In soil where plenty of rhizobia live, you can pull up a legume plant and easily find the nodules on the roots. The nodules vary in size from about a pin head to a little larger than a BB. Scientists say nodules that are red or pink inside are the best nitrogen fixers. They believe a comparatively smaller number of large nodules produce more nitrogen than a large cluster of small nodules.

Scientists have found that strains of rhizobia vary in their effectiveness as nitrogen producers. Also there seems to be a specific strain of the bacteria for almost every kind of legume. Today, you can buy inoculant that contains strains developed especially for the legume you intend to plant.

Inoculants are marketed either in liquid or powder form or as frozen liquid concentrate. In some cases commercial growers can buy seed that has been preinoculated with a special inoculant that can keep the bacteria alive on the exposed seed for a couple of months. As a gardener or small organic farmer, you will find the powdered inoculant best for your purposes. The "powder" is humus—reconstituted peat soil usually. Packed in moisture-sealing plastic bags or packets, the humus nurtures the bacteria in the inoculant and keeps it healthy if storage temperature does not get above 70° F. and the package is not left to dry out in direct sunlight. Extended periods of high temperature and sunlight kill the bacteria.

When you are ready to plant the seed, mix the inoculant into it according to the directions. Usually this entails sprinkling the powder over the seed and stirring the mixture until at least a speck or two of the inoculant adheres to each seed. Usually enough moisture remains in the inoculant packed in plastic bags or in coated tin or cardboard cans so that the powder will stick readily to the seed. If it doesn't, sprinkle a little water over the seeds and mix in the inoculant. If your inoculant has been stored properly beforehand, the bacteria could stay alive about two to three weeks on the unplanted seed. But try to plant the seed as soon as possible after inoculating, preferably right away, so that the bacteria enter the ground in good vigorous condition.

That's all there is to it. You may or may not see strikingly visible results in the legume crop you're growing. Legumes don't always respond right away to any kind of fertilization. But rest assured that the rhizobia are working. And the crop you plant next on that field may grow surprisingly well with no added nitrogen.

Other kinds of bacterial soil activators include compost starters which are added to compost heaps to aid in decomposition of organic matter. Organic serums on the market are applied as seed coatings or make a solution into which roots of transplants are dipped before being set in the ground. The serums are supposed to increase plant vigor and crop yields. Other activators contain bacteria which hasten breakdown of chemical residues in the soil. Still other products, with claims marvelous enough to tax the most vivid imagination, are applied as foliar sprays to stimulate better growth. Your decision whether to use any of these products will depend on how you answer the question: "Is it worth the cost?" As I have said, you can always try a little and see what happens. In the case of a growing crop, don't base your judgment on how vigorously the treated plant seems to be growing compared to the untreated. Wait and measure yields from both plants.

Rock Mineral Products

Most of the soil conditioners and fertilizers in this category have been discussed already—rock phosphate, granite dust, potash rock—I suppose even greensand goes in this group. Along with limestone, rock minerals form part of the basic organic soil nutrition program, complementing the organic matter in the soil in a most beneficial way.[22]

Calphos is a conditioner-fertilizer you don't hear mentioned often, though it has been used a long time. Rich in natural phosphates, it is usually blended into organic fertilizers where a quick-acting phosphate is desired.

Lithonia granite (sold under the brand name Hybro-Tite) is another rock product long used by organic growers. This gneiss rock is mined from deposits in Georgia and contains about 70 percent silica, 5 percent potash, 14 percent alumina, 1 percent lime, 4 percent soda, and 1 percent iron oxide. Like all rock minerals, it contains traces of many other minor elements.

Gypsum is one of the oldest soil conditioners still in use—even the redoubtable Ben Franklin is supposed to have argued its benefits. But most serious organicists won't use it, since they consider the sulfate in it to be harmful to the soil. Gypsum is controversial for other reasons among nonorganicists too. Many agronomists consider it next to worthless on most land east of the Mississippi where soil alkalinity is not a problem. But some farmers in the East use gypsum in place of lime because they think some of their land has been overlimed in the past.

Seaweed Derivatives

Seaweed fertilizers have held high interest for gardeners ever since Clemson University researchers found that seaweed extracts not only produced more vigorous growth but also seemed to protect plants from insects. Commercial growers have in some instances corroborated this evidence. One large-scale vegetable grower in Ohio achieved considerable insect control without toxic insecticides, a success he attributes in large measure to the use of seaweed fertilizers and sprays. One of the biggest orchard operations in Pennsylvania found a few years ago that seaweed sprays inhibited the activity of mites.

Seaweed and kelp extracts are rich in trace elements —Norwegian seaweed containing traces of about sixty of them. You can buy seaweed fertilizers in liquid undiluted or granulated forms. Seaborn, Maxicrop, and Sea Crop are some of the brand names you're likely to see advertised.

While there's no question about the organic nature of these products, they're expensive. Maxicrop is selling in California (in 1974) for about fifteen dollars for a fifty-pound bag or $8.50 for an eleven-ounce can of soluble powder. If you only need a small amount for a small garden, that's not so bad. And remember, if you buy an undiluted liquid, the bottle may last longer than you think. When I first started gardening in earnest, I bought a gallon of Seaborn. I don't remember what it cost, but it seemed expensive. But I found I had to mix only a small amount of it at a time with water. That gallon lasted three years.

Humates

This group of soil conditioners is receiving much publicity right now—and perhaps because of that it is also generating the most controversy. Humates certainly aren't new. The Indians of the Southwest were using them to fertilize corn crops in their droughty region when Indians on the East Coast were showing white men how to fertilize corn with fish heads. White men mimicked the southwestern Indians too for awhile, but mostly abandoned humates when commercial fertilizer became so convenient to use. Now that this convenience comes with a much higher price tag, some growers are taking another look at humates.

Humates are deposits of mineralized organic matter much like coal. They are high in humus—"fossilized humus" as some distributors call it—and well-endowed with traces of minor elements. The brand I tested this year was gray-black, coarsely ground so that it would flow freely through a fertilizer spreader. According to the label, the product contains no nitrogen, phosphorus, or potash to speak of, but lists a 6 percent calcium, 2 percent magnesium, and 1 percent sulfur content—ingredients you could get in limestone or gypsum. The product is described as a "glacial humus, deposits of which contain nature's own organic substances and minerals"—about 30 percent organic matter on the average, some thirty or more known trace elements, plus bacteria. Among these, the label lists minute quantities of boron, chlorine, cobalt, copper, iron, manganese, molybdenum, sodium, and zinc—about what you'd expect to find in a good organic soil already. The cost was five dollars for a fifty-pound bag (cheaper if bought in quantity), or about the same price as ordinary garden fertilizer. In my test plots on exceptionally rich soil, corn fertilized with the conditioner grew and yielded as well as corn fertilized with regular chemicals or only with the organic matter and fixed nitrogen from two preceding years of soybeans. The year was too dry for any kind of worthwhile comparison and none of the corn was very good. If I learned anything, it was that in a very dry year, organically grown crops on rich soil will do as well as crops fertilized with any kind of fertilizer or conditioner.

Some commercial farmers are using humates to prevent leaching of chemicals in their light soils. By building up organic matter with humates, they feel they can reduce chemical application appreciably, sometimes as much as 50 percent. For the organicist, the humates may be advantageous as a source of trace elements—if your soil is deficient. Some humates have a high pH, some a low pH. Be sure to check this point before using. You don't want to put a conditioner with a high pH on land that is already alkaline.

Soil Amendments Made from Composted Tree Bark

In addition to mulches already discussed, there are a number of fairly new products on the market made from ground-up, composted tree bark, which can be used as mulch, conditioner, and fertilizer. The amendments are certainly organic and worth serious consideration where available. Tree bark is richer in nutrients than leaves or sawdust. It makes an excellent organic potting soil.

Some of the bark composts have other organic fertilizers mixed into them. Barsola (NOMCO, Watertown, N.Y.), for example, contains dried poultry manure and other fertilizing ingredients. Other products contain bark only, such as Bambé (North Stratford, N.H.) which is composted from pure hardwood barks.

Other Dried, Processed Organic Fertilizers

As the price of chemical fertilizers rises, organic plant food, which has always cost more, may become more competitive. This trend should encourage the production and marketing of more organic fertilizers as convenient as Bovung and other dried manures like

Chic Green (3-4-2 analysis), or Milorganite (6-3-0) and other processed sludges.[23] I just discovered "F & B's All and Only 100% Natural Organic Garden Food" (Faesy & Beshoff, Inc., Edgewater, N.J. 07020). Sounds like a title of a Tom Wolfe short story. All and Only 100% Natural Organic Garden Food is a blend of bone meal, dried blood, cottonseed meal and cottonseed hull ashes, with an analysis of 5-5-5. Shur-Gro is another all-organic fertilizer (Canton Mills, Inc., Minnesota City, Mn. 55959) sold widely in labelled analyses—a 10-6-4, a 4-2-10, and others.

For the house plant grower, fish emulsion fertilizers offer another convenient way to get organic nitrogen, if not other nutrients. For instance, Atlas Fish Emulsion Fertilizer (Renton, Wis.), which I just noticed in a garden store, carries a guaranteed analysis of 5-1-1 and costs $1.69 a pint. But that's undiluted and must be mixed with water before using. Another source of nitrogen you can buy from the better organic supply stores is Agrinite, which is about seven percent N. It's a mixture of leather dust and tankage. Some stores also carry guano with an analysis of 12-3-1.

Finally, there are what I call the "true" soil conditioners—products made solely for the purpose of improving the tilth or physical consistency of the soil with no claims of adding fertility. These products seem to come and go—about once every five years they make a big splash of publicity and then fade away for awhile. Krilium, highly touted in the 1950s but ignored today, is a good example. No fertility value was claimed for Krilium, only its capability to improve soil structure and control erosion. Some products are made to keep clay soils from crusting, others to increase water absorption properties of a soil, others to increase permeability. A soil well-managed with organic methods won't need any other conditioning.

Chapter 12

Green Manure:
Grow
Your Own Fertilizer

Green manuring is a slightly old-fashioned term for the practice of growing certain grass and legume crops specifically for plowing, disking, or rotary-tilling them into the soil to improve tilth and fertility. Widely practiced for centuries, green manuring fell into disuse among modern farmers when chemical fertilizers became cheap and easily available. Now that commercial fertilizers are expensive, with their supply tied to the here-today, gone-tomorrow availability of fossil fuels, scientists are reconsidering green manuring. If present green manure crops can use solar energy directly and at no cost to add that much fertility to the soil, maybe man can develop even better ones that will add more nutrients to soil than we dream possible right now. After all, the reserve of carbonates in the earth and atmosphere that plants can convert to carbohydrates by photosynthesis is almost inexhaustible. Just as significantly, there is an equally inexhaustible supply of nitrogen in the atmosphere that legumes can draw on to convert to plant nitrogen in the soil for the all-important process of protein synthesis. All man has to do is grow the green manure crop and stand back and watch.

Organic gardeners and farmers have always relied on green manures for increasing fertility, especially on larger gardens and fields where heavy mulching and composting would be impractical. But green manuring can be adapted to any size operation. It's the least-labor way to add organic matter and also the easiest way to provide a vegetative shield over the land during winter to pre-

The clovers are among the best green manure crops you can grow. And there's a clover suitable for most every region. The gardener can turn in the whole crop for enormous benefits in soil fertility. The homesteader can remove several hay crops before turning in the clover for the same fertility benefits.

vent erosion. That's why green manures are often referred to as "cover crops."

Besides those advantages, each of the two kinds of green manures, nonlegumes and legumes, has its own particular advantages. Nonlegume cover crops, mostly grasses, are used for short-term production of organic matter. For instance, rye is sown in the fall and plowed under the following spring. In this way, land is not tied up with the green manure crop during the growing season. Also, the grass growing in the fall can "consume" and "store" in its fibers the available nitrogen in the soil which might otherwise leach out over winter.[24]

Legumes: The Best Green Manures

But legumes, and particularly the clovers, have far more advantages and are preferred for green manure whenever they can be used (by clovers, I mean alfalfa and sweet clover in addition to the true clovers: red clover, white clover, alsike clover, crimson clover, and the others). Here's why.

> 1. Clovers are good "foragers" and will find moisture and food where many other plants languish.
> 2. Clover roots grow deep into the soil and bring up minerals to the surface where other plants can use them.
> 3. Because of this root vigor, clover aerates the soil and improves drainage.
> 4. In built-up soil, clovers grow well enough to provide a crop of hay and still have second growth for a good green manure crop.
> 5. Beneficial teas can be made from clovers, not to mention sprouts from the

seeds—especially alfalfa seeds.

6. Clovers, particularly the white clover, are one of the best sources of nectar from which bees make honey.

7. Clovers insure rotation of crops in garden and field. This point is particularly important to gardeners who do not want to use pesticides. By taking a small part of the garden out of production of vegetables, fruits, and grains each year on a rotating basis, you are more apt to avoid build-up of insects and fungal diseases.

8. Clover breaks down readily in the soil, its nutrients becoming available to other plants quickly.

9. Best of all, clovers have the ability, already mentioned, to convert nitrogen in the air into nitrogen for plants. Actually, it is bacteria in the soil that make the conversion, but the legume plant is a necessary step in the process. When the bacteria come into contact with the clover roots, they enter the root hairs where they form tiny nodules. The biggest nodules I've ever found on clover roots were about ⅛ inch in diameter. As the bacteria feed the plant nitrogen, they receive other food from the plant and multiply rapidly. The symbiotic relationship produces an excess of nitrogen. It is this biologically "fixed" nitrogen, as scientists call it, which can be part of the answer to the problem of nitrogen fertilizer shortage.

(To take best advantage of this ability of legumes, the seed should be inoculated before planting, as explained under "Bac-

terial Inoculants" in the previous chapter. The person that sells you the seed
can sell you the proper inoculant.)

How much nitrogen can a clover crop "fix" in the
soil for subsequent crops? Science doesn't know yet
what the limits might be. What we know for sure is
that a good clover crop turned into the ground just
before bloom stage can add at least 150 pounds of
actual nitrogen to the soil per acre—that's equivalent
to about five tons of manure. Alfalfa will fix 175 to
225 pounds of nitrogen per acre, according to tests at
the University of Kentucky.

A clover hay crop that yields three tons of dry hay
per acre returns to the soil, if plowed under, over 100
pounds of potash per acre, sixty pounds of phosphorus,
and 100 pounds of nitrogen. I. P. Roberts, in a book
written nearly a century ago, called *Fertility of the Land,*
asserted that a garden should be sown on August 1 to
clover instead of being allowed to grow up in weeds.
By November 1, he reported, the clover would contain
over 100 pounds of nitrogen in tops and roots. Not all
that nitrogen would be available in the spring, but the
figure is quite astounding when you remember that a
100 pound sack of chemical fertilizer containing ten
pounds of actual nitrogen has been selling recently for
eight to ten dollars.

The only difficulty in using clover to improve soil
fertility is that you may have a problem getting a good
stand when you plant it on poor land. Sort of a Catch
22—you need the clover to improve the land and you
need to improve the land to get the clover! But if you
have followed the advice thus far given in the book—
drained your soil and limed it well—you should have
little trouble. Most clovers will grow promptly if soil
is not wet and not acid. On a garden that has grown
vegetables satisfactorily, you should be in good shape.

Starting a Green Manure Program

To start a green manuring program, you first should develop a rotation plan for your garden in order to have a portion of the garden in clover every fourth year. If you can divide the garden into four equal parts you can establish a four year rotation that is fairly easy to follow: two years vegetables, one year grain, one year clover. Or two years vegetables, one year strawberries, one year clover. Or one year vegetables, one year strawberries, one year small grain, one year clover. Or three years vegetables, one year clover. Any of these combinations will work.

Why grain in the garden, you might ask. Simply because, as more gardeners are finding out, growing wheat (or rye, barley, or even oats) in the garden is an easy and practical way to get your own organic, wholegrain flour for wholesome bread and breakfast foods. You can grind it in your blender. What's more, wheat makes an excellent "nurse crop" for the clover. The wheat is sown in the fall and the clover is planted in it in early spring. The wheat is harvested that summer and the clover grows vigorously afterwards. The nurse crop is not necessary to the establishment of the clover, but as farmers learned long ago, it is more economical—you get a cash grain crop from the land while the clover is growing.

Many clovers can also be planted in August if moisture is adequate. You can tear up an old strawberry patch in July, rotary-till it once or twice and, after a rain soaks the ground in early August (hopefully), plant. For many gardeners that rotation—strawberries to clover to two years of vegetables—may be more suitable and certainly just as economical as the wheat to clover to two years of vegetables rotation.

Sowing the Seed

Sowing clover seed on a garden does not require special equipment. Just inoculate the seed as previously explained, then scatter it as evenly as you can with your hand. Handle it carefully because the stuff is very expensive—around seventy-five dollars a bushel and fluctuating. But a little goes a long way; a bushel of seed weighs about sixty pounds. Alfalfa sown at a rate of ten to fifteen pounds per acre is adequate and most other clovers at a rate of twelve to fifteen pounds per acre will be adequate for a green manure crop. Remembering that there are almost 44,000 square feet in an acre, a plot 100 feet by 100 feet would be a little less than a fourth of an acre. Three pounds of alfalfa or red clover would cover it. A plot 50 feet by 50 feet would take one-fourth of that amount, and so forth.

On larger plots of ground—over an acre in size— use some kind of mechanical seeder. There are small, inexpensive broadcasters that strap to your back and there are large ones which attach to, and are powered by, tractors. For spring planting, broadcasting the seed on top of the ground works fine. For late summer planting, a regular drill-seeder that puts the seed in the ground, covers and packs it, is far better if you can borrow or rent one. If not, broadcast the seed on well-worked soil, then harrow the field to cover the seed. A cultipacker following the harrow and firming the soil will insure a good catch. On a small garden plot, you can rake soil over the summer-broadcast seed and get the same effect. Then firm the soil with a lawn roller if you have one.

When clover is sown in the spring, as it usually is in the North, a quiet morning in February or early March is the best time. The seed can be broadcast right on top of the snow. That way you can see where the seed falls and when you miss a spot. The melting snow carries the seed into the mud of the thawing field where it eventually germinates and roots.

I think a better time to sow the seed is after the snow is gone, with land freezing at night and thawing during the day. The surface of the earth is slightly pitted if you look closely. Broadcast the tiny clover seeds then and they fall into those small iced-mud fissures. When the mud thaws, it flows together, covering the seed.

Don't try to broadcast the seed if the wind is strong. Even a mildly strong wind can blow your seed from where you want it to fall.

Cutting: For Mulch or Hay

Spring-planted clover doesn't grow much until the nurse crop—wheat or whatever—is harvested. When the grain is cut, the young clover plants will often be clipped off, too. This won't hurt them, but avoid cutting the grain stalks close to the ground, if possible until August. At that time, you can mow the clover and whatever remains from the grain stalks, leaving the clippings on the soil as mulch and fertilizer. The clover will now grow back rank and green. When winter comes it will die and cover the soil with a protective layer of organic matter that eventually rots into the soil. If you are counting, you have already made two applications of fertilizer and organic matter with that clover. In the spring, the clover will grow again. Just before it blossoms, you can plow it under, or rotary-till it into the soil. But it's better for the soil to let it grow, mow it, and leave the clippings on the land. Farmers generally make hay out of that "first cutting" and you can too, if you have rabbits, a pig, cow or horse—all of which like dried clover hay.

After cutting red clover and most other clovers except alfalfa, they will make only one more strong regrowth during the year. (Alfalfa will make two or three.) By September this second growth will blossom and go to seed. Farmers will often harvest the seed with a combine either to sell or to sow for the next crop. Harvesting the clover seed takes little of the clover's nutritional value away from the land, as the clover stems and leaves are scattered back on the ground by the combine. If you aren't interested in the seed (for a garden, likely as not you won't be, unless you want your own seed for sprouting), you can plow under that second growth in the fall, or any time during the winter when and if the ground is fit to plow or spade or rotary-till, or in the following May after regrowth has begun.

Alfalfa can be kept growing productively for any number of years, unlike red clover, so you don't have to

Turning in a green manure crop can be a tiring job. At the least, a big tiller is required, with multiple passes doing the best job of incorporating the green matter in the soil. Where the garden area is expansive, a tractor-drawn plow may be the best tillage device to use.

plow it under the second year after planting if you don't want to. You can keep mowing and leaving it on the ground for mulch and soil enrichment. Or make a crop of hay out of it on alternate cuttings. Though the nutritive value of alfalfa is highest right before blossom stage, if you have bees and are not going to make hay, it's best to leave the alfalfa to go to bloom so the bees can harvest their crop, too. On red clover or alfalfa planted in late summer, do nothing except admire it the rest of the first year. In the spring, when it grows again, manage as I have described for the second year of spring planted seed.

Choosing a Legume for Your Region

I've mentioned only alfalfa and red clover, the two best legumes for green manure and nitrogen fixation in the North. There are many other legumes with advantages for specific areas:

Alsike clover will grow in the South but is more often planted (if at all) in the North. Its chief value is that it will stand a more acid and wet soil than most clovers. Sow six to ten pounds per acre.

Alyce clover, an annual legume of the lower South, needs good, well-drained land. Sow fifteen pounds per acre.

Bur clover is grown in the South and on the Pacific Coast. It will do better than red clover on poor soils in these regions. Plant in September.

Crimson clover is a common legume of the South. You see it growing along roadsides everywhere that the soil is not too acid. Plant in the fall, at least sixty days before frost, at the rate of fifteen pounds per acre.

Persian clover likes heavy moist soils in the South and milder Pacific Coast areas.

Sweet clover grows rankly just about anywhere except on acid soils. It's not much good for hay, but provides organic matter in great quantities. In fact, if allowed to grow to maturity, sweet clover is so thick and tall that it can be difficult to plow under. I don't recommend it, except where long and intensive cultivation has created a hardpan between topsoil and subsoil. Sweet clover roots will go through about anything.

All peas and beans are legumes—many of them are fine green manure crops. Just remember that the best results are obtained by inoculating the seeds before planting. The soybean is probably the best of all, but because it demands such a good price, no one would dream of plowing under a crop today. But in a garden, you might so dream. Grow a plot, harvest what beans you need for eating (we like to boil them while still green), then mow and till the green matter into the soil. Even when allowed to mature for a bean crop, the soybean fibers will return some organic matter and nutrition along with the added nitrogen the crop has fixed in the soil. On good land following three years of soybeans, I have raised good corn without any other fertilizer. In addition, soybeans seem to require little extra fertilizer to produce a good crop.

Plant soybeans in late spring at the rate of about a bushel (sixty pounds) per acre broadcast. Scatter the seed on top of worked ground, then rake or rotary-till lightly into the soil. Plantings can be made as late as July 10 in the North for green manure. Plow down in the fall. Many years soybeans will produce a seed crop though planted that late, even in the North. Where weeds are a problem, plant soybeans in rows so you can cultivate.

The cowpea is another good soil builder that will grow about anywhere. Handle the same as soybeans. On very poor ground, where clover is desired, plant a crop of cowpeas first, plow under, then sow clover.

The velvetbean is an annual for the South that will practically thrive on poor sandy soil. Sow after the soil has warmed up, broadcast or in rows. In rows—this holds true for soybeans and cowpeas too—the planting rate is about half that when the seed is broadcast or about twenty-five pounds per acre.

Certain members of the vetch family of legumes make good cover crops, hairy vetch in the North and Hungarian vetch in the South. I doubt if you'll find vetch any advantage over clover in the garden, however. Since it matures the same time as wheat, it is considered a weed in small grain crops.

The *Encyclopedia of Organic Gardening* mentions other legumes which you should know, at least the names, even if you don't have an occasion to use them. For instance, Hairy Indigo in the South makes a good strong summer growth despite (or because of) the hottest weather. Kudzu is another legume, though a perennial that can become a pesky weed. Fenugreek, sesbania, crotolaria, berseem, and black medic are other legumes, all but the last strictly southern in habitat.

Among lesser clovers you should be aware of, particularly in the North, don't forget white clover, the small clover of our yards. White clover goes on, drawing nitrogen into the lawn soil for the benefit of the bluegrass, year after year, yet rarely gets any praise. Except from the bees. Some people think white clover is unsightly in the lawn; I think it looks fine. Wherever it flourishes the bluegrass will too. Given lime, the plucky little clover is practically indestructible.

Mammoth clover, lespedeza, dalea (or Wood's clover), bird's-foot trefoil, and ladino clover are other legumes each of which (especially the last two) has a champion for one reason or another. I can't speak for the South because I haven't socked a hoe in the ground south of Kentucky, but from there on north, let me whisper in your ear: grow alfalfa if you can. If you can't, grow red clover. If that won't grow, improve your drainage, plow under a crop or two of green soybeans, throw on some more lime, and try red clover again.

Green Manure Grasses

Among nonleguminous plants that make good cover crops and green manure, rye and rye grass are at the top of the list. Sudangrass, brome, rape, oats, millet—any vigorous growing grass will make green manure, but rye is the best one.[25] Use it unless it doesn't grow for you. Only then try one of the others. (Rye seed is usually cheaper, too).

Another green manure crop you should try is buckwheat. It's not a legume nor a grass, but it seems able to grow on hard clays. Through root action, it loosens the soil to where it can be worked more easily, and its blossoms are good honey sources for bees too. Once you have tasted your own buckwheat cakes, you'll need no other excuse to grow the plant. I sow it broadcast in the same manner as I would the other crops. Buckwheat, however, should be planted in midsummer (July 4). It makes a crop in a hurry, before frost, and is often used as a second crop in a double-cropping system. You can plant it after any crop harvested before the middle of July.

Chapter 13

Soil Cultivation

After you have seen to it that your soil receives adequate amounts of air, water, organic matter, and nutrients, you have one more skill to master—the actual tilling of the soil—before you can call yourself the "compleat gardener." The better you have accomplished those former tasks, the easier soil tillage becomes. In fact, with a well-drained soil high in organic matter, you can pull some pretty dumb cultivation mistakes without adverse effects.

Some gardeners on light rich soils don't cultivate at all, relying on high organic matter to provide a good seedbed, and mulch to control weeds. But most gardens and all large fields require some cultivation. How much often depends on the type of soil and the objectives of the gardener or farmer. You would think that after centuries of tilling the soil, man would by now have settled upon a "best" way to prepare the ground for seed germination and plant growth, but that's far from true. There is as much controversy about tillage methods as over any other aspect of gardening and farming. One tool causes soil erosion while another compacts the soil. Very often, the problem lies not with the tool, but with its operator. Furthermore, faults ascribed to the tools are more often the faults of poor soil management. Any tool used on soil of low organic matter is going to cause problems.

The Fundamentals of Soil Cultivation

To make any cultivating tool work well (including hand tools), you need to understand *why* you cultivate, *when* you should cultivate, and *how* you should cultivate.

The most important reason for cultivating is to prepare a firm seedbed. When seed is placed in the soil, the dirt should fit around it snugly, so that moisture is readily available to germinate the seed. If you drop a seed among clods, it will just lie there until rain falls. If you drop a seed among loose, partially broken clods, the seed may germinate and sprout, but then the seedling dries out and dies if rain doesn't fall.

A second important reason for cultivation is weed control. While you cultivate for weed control, the soil benefits by being loosened for better aeration and drainage.

When to cultivate is usually the most difficult lesson for the novice gardener to learn. Soil moisture and temperature are the two gauges in determining the proper time to work soil—when the soil is "fit," as a farmer would say. Of these two considerations, soil moisture is the more crucial—if you work soil when it is too wet, especially clay soil, you work up a nice hard problem for yourself.

I like to tell gardeners mystified by soil "fitness" to spend a day making mud pies with their kids. Making mud pies gives you a "feel" for soils. Fill a bowl with sand, another with sandy loam, another with clay loam, and a fourth with clay. Mix water with each kind of soil in varying amounts and stir it around. Make mud balls. If you make a ball of wet sand, it falls apart. A ball of sandy loam falls apart with very light pressure. A handful of clay loam moistened and squeezed will hold its shape easily and crumble apart under pressure, depending on how wet it is, how hard you press it into a ball, and how much clay is present. When a mud ball crumbles apart easily and is not sticky to your skin, the ground has the proper amount of moisture in it so that it can be plowed, disked, hoed, or rotary-tilled easily. If the mud ball does not crumble in your fist, but is sticky, elastic, rubbery or slippery, the ground is too wet to work.

Make some mud pies out of all four kinds of soil and let them dry in the sun. The sand pie falls apart—won't make a pie, in fact. The sandy loam may stick together, but just barely. The clays, on the other hand, "bake" to a hardness corresponding with the amount of clay present—the more clay and the less organic matter present, the harder. In making a clay mud pie, you have essentially worked the soil too wet. If you try to stir your garden soil under similar moisture conditions, it too will "bake" in the sun to hard clods.

Now go back to your dry mud pies. Break one of them up—with a hammer if necessary. Soak a second one in water for about five minutes and set it out to dry again. Do nothing, for the moment, with a third pie. Note how the pie breaks up. Depending upon how much clay and organic matter are present, the pie may break up easily or with great difficulty. Most likely the latter will be the case, since the stirring with water and compaction in making the mud pie jammed the clay particles

193

even more tightly than normal against each other. Visualize this clay pie as the soil in your garden if worked too wet. How many times would you have to go over it with tiller, hoe, or disk, to work up a good seedbed? You might not be able to do it at all because the numerous workings of the soil would finally reduce it to a powder rather than a loose granular consistency, just as you reduce the clay pie first to pebble-like consistency and then to powder if you keep on trying to break it up.

Powdery, overworked soil is just about as bad as the clods of wet-worked soil. Rain on that powdery clay can turn the soil surface into a crust almost as hard as asphalt. Soil crusting can be reduced and eventually eliminated by raising organic matter content to 5 percent or more. But the gardener (or farmer) who insists on working clay soil too much—into a fine powder—will always have crusting problems and a crust prevents good seedling emergence.

Remember that we left one mud pie unscathed. Hopefully, it will be a good hard one, maybe almost hard enough to bake into pottery in a kiln. Just let it sit outside over winter on top of some bare ground, so that it will freeze and thaw a couple of times before spring. Then, in April, after the warm winds of spring have blown the soil dry, step on that mud pie. Cut through it with a hoe. Or disk. Or tiller. Almost always, you will find that it breaks up easily into nice granular soil.

What you are witnessing is one of the principles involved in the fall plowing of clay soils. Winter freezing mellows soils so that they can be worked easily into a seed bed. Furthermore, having turned the soil over in the fall, loosening it from the subsoil, the surface dries out quicker than it would have if left unplowed. All this means that if you have tough clay soil, till it in the fall for easier spring cultivation—and if you till it when it's a little too wet, don't worry too much because winter freezes will overcome the mistake.

Whether fall plowing or spring plowing is "better" is a source of continuing argument among farmers, though not as much as formerly. Today, most commercial farmers have so much land to plow they start right after fall harvest and keep on going, as long as the weather permits, fall, spring, and winter too to finish in time for spring planting. For gardeners and farmers with a choice, the main advantage of fall tillage, in addition to what has already been said, is that it does spread out the workload. Ground spaded at leisure in late fall is ground you don't have to spade in haste in the spring.

Organic growers, however, will do most of their plowing in the spring, to take advantage of the spring growth of their green manure crops. Spring plowing also seems to result in a seedbed freer of weeds than is the case with fall-plowed ground.

In fall tillage, the surface of the soil is left rough to resist wind and water erosion. But with spring tillage, it is better to work the soil soon after plowing. Otherwise, if rainfall is scanty or a spring-summer drought follows, you can lose the moisture that was stored in that spring-turned soil. By working the surface, the finer soil produced on the surface will hold moisture in. If you *knew* rain would follow plowing, you wouldn't need to work the ground right away—in fact, it would be better not to—but who can predict the weather with such assurance?

Soil temperature is critical not to cultivation but to germination. Few seeds will germinate if soil temperature three inches below the surface is lower than 55° F. and won't germinate well if the temperature is below 60° to 65° F. Normally soils warm up in spring as they dry, so that if the soil is dry enough to work, it will also be warm enough to plant. But not always. Drier than usual early springs can lure a gardener into planting too early. If cold wet weather follows, the seed rots rather than germinates.

Hand Tools

For the smallest gardens, hand tools are more appropriate than power tools and much more economical. How big is smallest? My own limits on size of garden for handworking are from 2,000 square feet for older folks to as much as 3,000 square feet for young vigorous gardeners who need the exercise anyway. For such gardens, the best plow is a spade, the best disk is a hoe, and the best harrow is a steel garden rake. In addition, a hand-pushed cultivator can be purchased for less than fifty dollars that always starts with the first push, uses no fuel at all, and will last a lifetime.

For a small garden, you need only hand tools for successful cultivation. The spading fork and the spade will "till" the soil. The pick comes in handy for sun-baked clays, but wielding the rake to gather leaves to mulch the soil the previous fall will almost eliminate the need for the pick.

196

Turning the Soil

To turn the soil over, a spading fork is usually better than a round-pointed shovel, though both are adequate. Spading soil in the traditional manner has become almost a ritual, and so like most traditional rituals, is honored more in print than in practice. Using a ditch a foot deep and about a foot and a half wide, the spader laboriously transferred soil from the top six inches of the trench to the bottom of the trench already dug. The bottom six inches then went on top of the preceding trench. Going across the whole garden in this manner, one effectively reversed the whole top foot of soil. Where topsoil is twelve inches deep, deep-digging in this manner would be beneficial to tight soils. However, over much of the United States, and I assume elsewhere, topsoil is eight inches deep at the most, and deep-digging would only throw subsoil on top of the ground. In this situation, the industrious gardener is supposed to loosen the bottom six inches of soil of his spading trench with his spading fork, but not lift it out.

The way most people spade is somewhat easier than double-digging or deep-digging. First, you dig a trench about the depth of your shovel blade or fork tines (the depth to which you can easily plunge your spade). The dirt you dig out is put in the wheelbarrow and wheeled to the other end of the plot you are going to spade. You'll need that dirt there to fill your last trench.

Next, simply dig another trench next to the first one, turning the dirt a spadeful at a time, upside down into that first trench. You'll find it's hard to turn the soil completely upside down. Don't worry. Just bury the plant residues that were on top of the soil, especially if you're spading sod. I usually tip my spadeful of dirt on its side rather than completely upside down. That leaves the plant residues and other organic matter that were on the soil surface at all depths of the spaded dirt rather than buried completely at the bottom of the trench. I believe the organic matter rots faster that way.

Proceed across the garden in the same fashion, spading, turning, spading, turning. Don't get in a hurry and take too big a bite. That will only tire you faster. Keep the spading side of your trench straight up and down. In sod, the grass mat on top of the soil will make spading more difficult. You will try to lift a spadeful and find it is still attached to unspaded ground by the grass roots. Use a round-pointed shovel in sod rather than a spading fork and the shovel will cleave the roots better. At the edges of the plot to be spaded, I always mark a line and then go along the length of that line with the shovel, jamming it down about four inches to slice through the

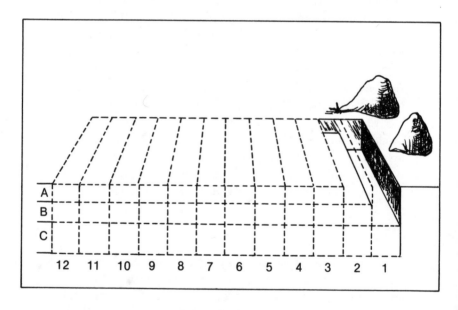

Triple spading is the ideal: the garden soil is carefully spaded and mixed. The top layer (A) is removed from blocks 1 and 2 and saved for eventual use in blocks 11 and 12. Soil is next removed from block 1B and saved for use in block 12B. Next, 1C is spaded to loosen and turn the soil, 2B is moved to cover it, and 3A is used to top off block 1. The sequence continues until the entire garden has been spaded. The process is laborious, and in practice is seldom done.

grass roots. Then while you're spading, the shovelful along the edge will lift out easily. You also know by that fact that you *are* at the edge of the area you want to spade. You don't want to dig one spadeful more than you have to!

When you turn the soil over, give each spadeful a whack to crumble it or stick your shovel or fork into it and twist. Either maneuver breaks the clod a little and leaves the surface loose and friable.

If you are spading in the fall or early winter, you should leave the surface rough after spading. As with fall plowing, the rough soil surface will absorb and hold more water through winter and freezes will mellow it better. The soil will also dry out faster in spring. If, however, you are spading in spring or early summer, you should work the surface as soon as you can after spading, so that finer soil on the surface will hold soil moisture in. Don't work the soil deeply, though, as that will only drag sod or other plant residues which you have spaded under back on top of the ground.

Preparing a Seedbed

If you are sticking with hand tools, the hoe makes the best tool to begin the job of preparing a seedbed on fall-spaded soil. The hoe does the job a disk would do after plowing on a farm, or what the rotary tiller would do in a larger garden. Hoeing can be hard work, but you can cut in half the amount of effort you expend with the right technique. Do not chop with the hoe. Never raise your hoe any higher than your knees and rarely higher than the top of your ankle. Hoeing should be a *pulling* effort rather than a pounding or chopping action. The slant of the blade to the handle on a good hoe is designed so that if you set the hoe blade on the ground in front of you and pull the hoe towards you with a little downward pressure on the middle of the hoe handle, the hoe blade will go into the soil, breaking a two or three inch furrow as you pull. Take advantage of this "natural" action as you hoe your ground. Slice up a strip no more than twelve inches, measured forward from your toes. Keep the hoe blade on the backswing a couple inches above the ground, letting the blade bite into the soil a foot in front of you. Pulling it towards your toe, lift again, slicing up another swath of soil the width of your hoe. With this method, not only will you last longer but the hoe will too.

With the soil surface loosened by the hoe, go to work with the steel rake, smoothing and leveling the ground for planting. I try to stand on the edge of the garden plot, pushing and pulling the rake as far as I can reach, and raking off rocks, bits of wood, or sod chunks to the garden's edge out of the way. The rake will also break up any clods that remain and leave your soil ready to plant. The rake performs the same task the harrow does.

For row vegetables, next make your planting furrows in the raked ground with the corner of the hoe blade. Depth depends on what kind of seed you are planting. Half an inch is fine for most small vegetable seeds, up to two inches for corn and bean seed. If the soil is dry and especially for late plantings in summer, plant small seeds 1½ inches and larger ones three to 3½ inches deep, down where there's more moisture possibly available for seed germination.

Weed Control

Hand cultivation for weed control should begin three days after planting, *before* your seeds come up. Many gardeners do not understand the effectiveness of pre-emergent cultivation and don't know how to do it.

Watch the soil surface very closely after you have planted your seed. In about three days, you will notice (in most gardens) many tiny weeds beginning to sprout. A cursory cultivation *with the steel rake* will kill them without the expenditure of much muscle power. Just rake gently—over the whole planted space including the rows to about an inch depth. You won't hurt your seeds if you don't rake as deeply as you planted. You can rake across corn rows even when the plants are coming up if you are gentle about it. You may break off a spear or two of corn, but the amount of weeds you kill more than makes up for that.

I can't emphasize too much the importance of this preemergent rake cultivation. Before the days of herbicides every farmer kept ahead of weeds with this type of cultivation using an implement called the rotary hoe. For the garden, the rake works fine or you can use a small, hand-pushed rotary hoe made by True Temper called the "Soil Spur." I recommend going over the rows three to five days after planting, even if you can't see weeds germinating. In fact, if you continue the rake cultivation between the rows after your plants emerge (you can't, of course, rake over the small plants), you can get by with no other cultivation at all. And with a rake, you can weed very close to plants without harming them. Moreover, the rake cultivation is much faster than a hoe or push cultivator.

However, you can't rake soil when it is wet, so if rain falls after planting and the weather continues to be wet for long, the weeds grow. Once they are an inch tall, they can't be killed effectively with the rake or the rotary hoe. Then you must rely on your trusty hoe, or better, a good wheel-type push cultivator. Not only will the cultivator effectively control weeds between the rows, but, used intelligently, will throw enough dirt into the row of growing vegetables (after they are three inches or more above ground) to bury small germinating weeds there. That reduces the amount of hand weeding you have to do.

Generally, the larger the wheel on the push cultivator, the easier it is to push. Actually, I don't believe any small wheel cultivators are made anymore—and darn few large wheel kinds.

Rotary Tillers

If your garden gets too large for practical hand cultivation, and is too small to justify a large garden tractor or small farm tractor, what you need is a rotary tiller. The tiller replaces both spade and hoe, and can replace rake and cultivator too, with a little ingenuity. A tiller, run shallowly between rows, makes a weed cultivator without equal.

Because of its versatility, the tiller is probably the most popular garden tool made today. But to determine whether you can economically justify purchasing one, you should compare costs and the amount of food your garden produces. You can assume that a good tiller will cost at least $300 and probably more by the time you read this. I think it is foolish to buy one that is under-

In very large gardens a rotary tiller is useful for weed cultivation between rows. Adjust the machine so it moves quickly through the rows without digging too deeply into the soil.

horsepowered—six horsepower (HP) is fine, seven or eight better, five the absolute minimum. Models smaller than that will not give you much satisfaction. Another $50 to $100 for greater power and strength is money well spent.

So, figure a tiller at $300 to $500. Compare that to the cost of the hand tools it replaces: $6 for a round-pointed shovel or $5.50 for a spading fork; $4 for a decent hoe; $5 for a bow-type steel garden rake (don't get the cheapest rake when for a dollar or two more you can get one that will last a lifetime) or $6 for a dual-purpose steel rake with a set of flanged, extra-strong teeth to pulverize soil; and a cultivator, $40.

In sixty years of gardening, you will probably buy at least two spades, hoes, rakes, and one cultivator. That's $80, more or less, or a buck-thirty a year. In that time, you'll own perhaps five tillers for a total cost of at least $1,500, or $26 a year.

Obviously, if you are only going to raise $26 worth of food a year, you can't justify a tiller economically (though you may justify it as a recreational vehicle). In fact, by the time you add in other costs, you probably should be raising at least $75 worth of food to make a tiller "pay." And if you have a $500 to $600 tiller, make that $150. Now that food prices are as high as they should have been all along to pay for the real cost of our exorbitant use of fossil fuel and energy, raising $75 worth of food is not hard to do.

Another way to answer the question of how much production is necessary to justify a tiller is in terms of garden size. I don't know whose tables you use on food costs, but the only one I put much faith in is my wife's. She says that a family of four, eating the vegetables and fruits they *should* eat, will spend nearly $500 a year on these items alone, if they have to buy them all.

Relying on my experience, you need a half acre of ground to raise all your fruits or vegetables, though I realize a skilled gardener could do it all on a quarter acre. Compromising, I'll say ⅜ of an acre equals $500 of food at retail price. Then ⅛ of an acre equals $166 worth. Half of that (¹⁄₁₆ acre) equals about $80, below which economic justification of a tiller becomes questionable. And ¹⁄₁₆ of an acre just happens to be about all the land that it is pleasurable to work by hand—an area about 100 feet by twenty-seven feet.

Of course, really hard-working gardeners who need to economize as much as possible can work by hand as much as ⅛ of an acre per person and raise more food in that space than some of us do with a whole acre. Ask the Chinese. They can do much better than that.

But hoping to avoid arguments, let's say that when we softer Americans, holding down a full-time job elsewhere, increase our garden size beyond ¹⁄₁₆ of an acre to something closer to ⅛ of an acre, we'll need a rotary tiller. People handicapped physically in any way may need one regardless.

Most American garden tillers cut a swath about twenty inches wide. Models that attach to or are pulled by garden tractors cut up to thirty to thirty-six inches wide. England makes big tillers you walk behind, 12 HP and more, so well-balanced that you can handle them with ease. (If you can't find information on these anywhere, try the Geiger Company, Harleysville, Pennsylvania, a wholesale distributor of all kinds of horticultural equipment.) I've had no experience with these tillers, but I would think they would handle as much as five acres easily if you didn't mind the walking. However, most of the tillers commonly used in this country become inefficient once garden size or tillable land exceeds an acre or acre and a half because the tiller is too slow. Beyond an acre, you should start looking at the larger garden tractors and their equipment which we'll talk about a little later.

Tillers are either rear-mounted or front-mounted.

With a front-mounted tiller, you push down on the handles to make it dig deeper, the same as the rear-mounted, though the principles involved are different. When you sock the "brake" of the front-mounted tiller into the ground, the tiller can't go forward and the blade continues to turn in place, going deeper into the soil. If the soil is hard, the tiller blades will bounce off it, causing the vibrations that after an hour or two can tire you out. The rear-mounted tiller won't vibrate when the going gets tough, but if you try to force it to bite

Here's what a rotary tiller does that no other tillage device can: it efficiently mixes the soil and organic matter.

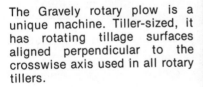

The Gravely rotary plow is a unique machine. Tiller-sized, it has rotating tillage surfaces aligned perpendicular to the crosswise axis used in all rotary tillers.

into tough soil, it will lunge ahead, dragging you with it. The moral of the story is that neither type works well in very hard soil or in heavy sod. Here, as elsewhere, patience is the answer. Go over the area several times, letting the blades chew into the ground only an inch or so at a time. In the case of sod, allow the soil surface to dry out some between passes with the tiller. After the first pass, you'll have a mess. Cut through the mess the second time at right angles to the first working. Don't try to till sod when the ground is hard and dry. Wait until spring.

The easiest way to till sod is not to try. Instead, cover the area with a foot of leaves in the fall and leave them there the whole next year. (You can set out plants, like tomatoes, down through the leaves if you want.) By the following fall, most of the leaves will have rotted away and the sod, too. Then you can rotary-till easily.

Tillers won't always cut up plant residues on the garden either. Things like tomato vines and cornstalks will tangle in the blades, especially if the blades have dulled with use. It's best to run a rotary mower over the patch to be tilled first if there's lots of plant material on it.

Tillers will "disk" plowed soil very well. If the plowed area had been in sod, do not let the tiller dig too deep as it will bring sod back to the surface. Tillers will fall-plow or spring-plow garden soil that has been previously cultivated and do an excellent job of it. They will incorporate into the soil chopped straw, hay, grass clippings, or leaves exceedingly well, and as mentioned, they will cultivate between rows too.

The Gravely cultivation system must be given special mention as there is nothing else quite like it, as far as I know. The Gravely walking tractor employs a front-mounted plow which works with a slanted horizontal movement rather than the vertical tiller blade movement. The machine does a good job of working up the soil and does better than a tiller on sod. If you buy a Gravely and intend to plow with it, be sure to get the optional gear system that provides an extra-slow low gear. In normal low gear, the tractor often moves too fast for plowing. The Gravely has a tiller attachment made strictly for cultivation after plowing and for weeding, not for digging the soil up as deeply as a regular tiller will.

Garden Tractors

When you have more than two acres of ground to cultivate every year, American rotary tillers become inadequate for the total cultivation job. (But don't get rid of your tiller. It will always come in handy for some situations.) For between two and four acres of ground to till, the most efficient machinery is the larger garden tractor and its accessories. Since you will no doubt need the tractor for mowing anyway, you can spread the cost of the tractor over both the lawn and field operations.

Americans have been brainwashed into riding whenever possible and walking only when it can't be avoided, rather than the other way around as it should be. We have, therefore, embraced the riding lawn mower with a fervor far beyond its merits, producing such absurd scenes as the overweight lot owner riding an undersized lawn mower, the bulk of the former nearly eclipsing the sight of the latter. The fellow could use a walking mower twice as good as that rider at half the price and do himself a tremendous physical favor, too. Walking would reduce his fatness and lessen the chances of back trouble or piles from sitting on that jolting, uncomfortable little rider. People get what they deserve every time.

Walking Tractors

At any rate, before you buy a $2,000 garden tractor

to cultivate your two or three acres, you might first look at some $1,000 walking tractors if you want to save money. (You can spend a lot more than that. As with tillers, the Europeans have gone in more for perfecting walking tractors than building toys for men to ride on. Large horticultural supply companies, like the previously mentioned Geiger Company, can tell you where to shop for them, but these tractors are often unavailable in parts of the U.S.) Walking tractors are usually rated around 8 HP but may need dual wheels to deliver that much power to their drawbars. They'll pull small single plows and cultivators similar to the ones that riding garden tractors can accommodate. The walking tractor's advantage over the riders is that it is much easier to maneuver between row crops.

Riding Tractors

However, if you can afford it and if you have a lot of lawn to mow too, the larger riding garden tractors have more power and do a better primary cultivation job. *Just remember that these tractors will not fit down between your rows for cultivating.* There are a few riding tractors (foreign) made especially for the commercial horticultural trade that are skinny enough to pass through wide row spacings, but most such spacings make inefficient use of space in American vegetable and row crop plantings.

What horsepower should you choose in a riding tractor? I say as big as you can afford, because the larger tractors (14 HP and up) have a much longer total life, are built tougher, and can be repaired and kept running longer. But the soil cultivating tools made for garden tractors will work adequately on a 10 HP model and some, even on an 8 HP model.

Instead of a spade, now you will use a plow; in place of a hoe, a disk; in place of a rake, a harrow. Several companies make these attachments for garden tractors, miniatures of the same equipment for farm tractors.

Most manufacturers of small implements market under their own brand name and/or through other outlets. Sears carries many such tools and so does Montgomery Ward. It's a common practice for some big tractor companies to sell the tools under their own brand name, even though they don't make the tools themselves. So, before you insist one small plow is better than another, better find out for sure if they were both made by the same company!

Small Plows

Plows are identified first of all by size, the small ones coming in eight-, ten-, and twelve-inch sizes. As a riding

Outgrow your tiller? Tired of walking? Garden tractors take the limp out of your step and the bulge out of your wallet. But for the big big garden, they are hard to beat tools. Rotary tillage attachments are available for most, as are farmlike plows, discs and harrows.

209

tractor attachment, only single plows, or "one-bottom" plows are sold. No garden riding tractor I know of can pull a double or "two-bottom" plow. The size refers to the plow's cutting width—an eight-inch plow cuts a furrow eight inches wide, and so forth. Cutting depth of a plow should be limited to about half the cutting width. An eight-inch plow should be adjusted to cut no more than four inches deep, and a twelve-inch no more than six inches deep. Better to get a larger plow and vary your cutting depth from year to year between four and six inches to avoid hardpanning. In heavy clay soils, farmers have found that plowing year after year at the same depth (especially with intensive cultivation that does not keep deep-rooted plants in rotation every three years), a somewhat impermeable layer of clay forms at plow depth. That's a hardpan. If you're gardening organically, you shouldn't have to worry about hardpans.

Because of the way a plow works, you just can't root the soil up any way you please. A plow lifts the soil from one place and deposits it eight to twelve inches to the side of its original position. The ditch that is left is called a furrow. After the first pass across the garden or field, the furrow ditch is there to throw the dirt over into from the second furrow and so forth. So when you are finished plowing, you will have at least one furrow left over. This is called a dead furrow. Naturally, the first time you plow across the field or garden, you do not have a furrow already there. So the dirt turned over by the plow blade falls on the normal surface, leaving a ridge of dirt. This ridge is called a headland. The art of plowing demands that in subsequent years of plowing, you make your headlands fall where last year's dead furrows were and last year's headlands become this year's dead furrows. If you don't do that, your field will become less level every year.

Just reading that, I doubt if you will understand what I mean. You have to have plowed a few years and been chewed out by your father for doing it wrong a couple of times. I'll try to draw it out for you. Here's the plot to be plowed—the most efficient shape is a rectangle twice as long as it is wide.

Leave enough room at each end for convenient turning, lifting the plow as you do. When the plowed section gets as close to the sides of the field as the furrows are to the ends of the field, then you plow around the whole field, including the turning area, until you are finished.

The next year, begin plowing in the opposite direction on the outsides of the field. Start at H, go to I, lift the plow and go to K, drop the plow and go to J, and so forth. You are now "throwing the ground out," whereas the previous year, you "threw the ground in." If you do not alternate in this fashion at each plowing, the dead furrows on the edges of the field would get deeper at each plowing, and the headland in the middle would get higher. Plowing properly, your dead furrow the second year will come in the middle of the field where your headland is the first year.

Visualize the diagram (p. 212) as representing a plot of ground no more than a 100 feet wide if you are plowing with a small plow. That's about all the bigger a plowing section (called a "land") should be, otherwise you'll be spending too much time turning at the ends. If your plot is larger than one "land," make two lands or more. H to I will then become a dead furrow equidistant between the first headland A-B, and another headland that you would strike out on the other side of H-I. (Just visualize another diagram like the one shown directly beneath it.) Then in the next year's plowing, your first headland would be struck out in the dead furrow H-I. Yes, you'll still be able to see the dead furrow, even though you have worked the ground and planted a crop over it. In fact, you don't want to obliterate the dead furrow completely by frequent diskings, because you

211

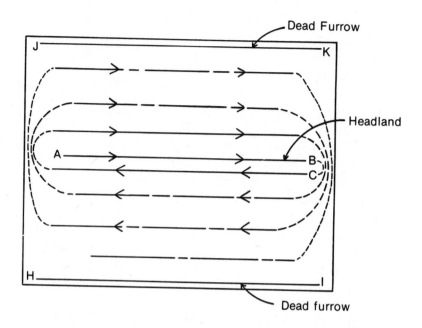

want that slight ditch across the field in which to throw the ground from your headlands the next year. Otherwise, the headlands would stick up too high from the surrounding soil.

I won't say any more. Go out and plow awhile. Then come back and read this. It'll make more sense then.

On small garden plots, you can ignore that information anyway because you can plow all one way and drive empty back the other way to avoid forming headlands and dead furrows. On larger plots, that would waste fuel and time.

The Disk

In small tractor equipment, you'll find the "single" disk and the "tandem" disk. The first consists of two sets of disks (or "gangs") in a single row with the two gangs slanted toward each other in a kind of "V" shape. A tandem disk has two more gangs behind the first two, slanted in the opposite direction. Pulling the disk straight forward while the gangs are slightly cocked is what causes the cutting and turning action of the disks in the soil.

As far as I'm concerned, the single disk is all but worthless. But the tandem disk is, on the other hand, one of the best cultivating tools at your disposal. In good organic soil, a disk can work the ground sufficiently without plowing at all (unless the field is covered with tough sod), and many organic farmers no longer use a moldboard plow at all. Instead, they use a heavy, large-disked version of the tandem disk called the offset disk, a tool not available for small garden tractors.

Since tandem disks for garden tractors may need extra weight, they are equipped with carrying frames above each gang. A cement block in each frame is plenty of extra weight. A half block may suffice, but sacks of dirt make good weights, too.

Small disks like the Brinly-Hardy DD-1000 cut a swath about thirty-two inches wide, and can be adapted to three-point-hitch systems for easier handling. You can vary the cutting depth of the blades by adjusting the slant of the gangs. It's important that the disk leaves a level swath of worked dirt. The back two gangs must be set to level the middle and side ruts which the front two gangs make. Don't be discouraged, on hard ground or ground covered with some plant residue or mulch, if the disk doesn't work up the ground well the first time over. On each additional trip, the tool will cut increasingly better.

But it's important not to overwork a piece of ground just because it's so much fun to disk. On clay soils, the disk would eventually break down the soil structure to a fine powder which would crust badly if a hard rain subsequently should fall.

The Harrow

No matter how well you adjust your disk, it will

leave a sort of rolling surface, hardly noticeable until you try to drive across the field at right angles to the way the disking went. To solve this possible problem, farmers pull some kind of "drag" or leveler" behind the disk to smooth out highs and lows. Most often, the drag is a form of harrow and the most common kind of harrow today, as always, is the spike-tooth harrow. Brinly-Hardy makes a good one for pulling behind small disks in that it extends a little behind the cutting width of the disk—necessary for good leveling.

Another type of harrow is the spring-tooth harrow: tandem sets of sharpened iron straps, bent in the form of a "C." There's nothing wrong with spring-tooth harrows except that on dirt that contains a lot of vegetable matter—as an organic soil no doubt would—the teeth act more like a rake than a soil worker and plug up with the mulch, straw, cornstalks, grass, or whatever you are trying to mix into your soil. Unless you shred all your old plant residues, the spring-tooth harrow won't work to your satisfaction.

After you have disked and harrowed your land, it should be ready to plant. About three days after your seeds are in the ground (before they come up) is time for the most important weed cultivation of all—as I've already described in the discussion on hand tools. This preemergent cultivation is especially crucial for organic farmers and gardeners who don't want to use herbicides. Let the weeds get the jump on your crop now and you may never get ahead of them.

The tool to use can be the spike-tooth harrow, with the teeth set very shallow so as not to dig your seed out. But a better tool is the rotary hoe—a set of curved-spike wheels that when pulled over the ground disturb sprouting weed seeds just enough to kill them without hurting your sprouting crops. In fact, the rotary hoe can be used to kill weeds even when your corn and beans are an inch above the soil. The tool will dig out some of your plants but not enough to hurt. And it will polish off another crop of sprouting weeds which you cannot otherwise cultivate mechanically until your garden and field plants are tall enough so shovel cultivators don't bury them with dirt.

Weed Cultivators

All kinds of cultivator sets are made for power tractors. They're just like the ones on push-wheel cultivators only much larger. They can come equipped with wide shovels (sweeps) or narrow shovels (diggers) and can be adjusted to straddle a row or cultivate between rows. Some cultivators can be used also as chisel plows. Brinly-Hardy's CC-600 cultivator, for example, is really a small chisel plow. The chisel plow, by the way, is a large tool that is used by some farmers in place of the moldboard plow to perform basic soil tillage. Chisel-plowed soil suffers less from wind and water erosion than moldboard-plowed soil. Chisel plowing is faster than moldboard plowing, but it requires big tractor power, which is why I make only passing reference to it (you aren't going to do it with garden-tractor or small farm-tractor power).

Another tool commonly used for breaking up clods is the cultipacker or soil pulverizer. It consists of a row or two rows of heavy steel wheels generally pulled behind a disk. Some cultipackers for large tractors have a set of spring-tooth harrows between the two sets of cultipackers, in which case the tool is called a cultimulcher. For garden tractors, this combination tool is not available. Some manufacturers sell a tool bar, however, upon which you can affix whatever soil-working or weeding tool you wish. Cultipackers are available for such tool bars. On good, organic soil, the cultipacker is seldom needed.

The cultipacker is also used to firm seed after broadcast planting (or even after drill planting) of grass seed.

215

The cultipacker, by pressing the seed into the ground and firming the soil over it, gives better germination than broadcasting alone. However, almost as good a result can be obtained from using a disk or rotary tiller lightly after broadcasting.

I've said little about planting itself, because that is not strictly a soil-working operation. However, it goes without saying that there are two ways to plant, by drilling and by broadcasting, the latter used for grass, hay, wheat, oats, and sometimes soybeans. Broadcasting can be done with no other tool than your hand, though it is quite difficult to get the seed spread evenly that way. Hand-operated broadcast seeders are still commonly available—the Cyclone brand is the one usually sold in catalogs and garden stores. The simplest kind are the horn broadcasters, which consist of a canvas seed bag that straps on your shoulder with a hole in the bottom through which the seed enters a long metal horn, big end first. The sower swings the horn back and forth in front of him horizontally as he walks, and the seed flies out the small end of the horn in an even pattern. Price is less than four dollars.

For about seven dollars more, you can buy a broadcaster that spreads the seed by a hand-cranked propeller attached to the canvas bag. The propeller throws the seed out evenly on the ground. There are three or four models of this broadcaster, one of which the catalog will describe as the "heavy duty" model. It costs about a dollar more but is well worth it.

With one of these broadcasters, a man can sow ten acres of clover on a quiet February morning. That's my very favorite farming job. It requires no fuel other than my calories, and the little broadcaster works so quietly, I can hear the seed hit the ground.

I also sow wheat, oats, and other small grains by hand this way. First, I disk the field well, broadcast the seed, then set the disk very shallow and go over the ground again—a process which will bury most of the seed an inch or two under the soil.

Heavier hand-cranked broadcasters are designed for spreading lime and fertilizer, in addition to seed. Next in size are wheeled broadcasters that you push, familiar to anyone who has a lawn to take care of, or larger models pulled by lawn and garden tractors. Many farm-sized broadcasters are made to run off the power take-off shaft of tractors.

The drill is the name of the grass and small grain seeder that injects seed directly into the soil and covers it. No small garden tractor drill is manufactured because broadcasting is so much cheaper, but on farms most small grains are sown with drills. I'm probably the only person in the cornbelt still broadcasting wheat—and, of course, I do only an acre. Drills do a much better job of planting than broadcasting. At least, drills are a surer way to get a good stand, especially in the absence of timely rains.

For planting vegetables in rows, manufacturers offer a great variety of planters including sophisticated replicas of the ancient dibble stick. These latter are hollow tubes with a box on them to hold the seed, and a triggered tripping mechanism that drops a seed or two when the tube is plunged into the soil. We used to call them "corn re-planters" when I was a kid, and many a hot June day I walked the cornfields with one of them, injecting kernels of corn into hills that had not come up at the first planting.

Enterprising gardeners sometimes devise simple planting tubes for themselves so they don't have to bend over and plant by hand. For about nine dollars (1974 prices) you can buy an adaptation of this tool—a tube with a wheel on it called the Plant-Rite Row Seeder. You find it in almost all garden catalogs. It's made for small, packet-at-a-time seeding.

For larger gardens, there's a variety of row seeders,

some pushed by hand at about thirty dollars each, and larger ones to pull with your garden tractor. The largest have two compartments, one for seed and one for fertilizer. Row planters should have a selection of interchangeable plates for different seed sizes. Prices range anywhere from seventy dollars to $300.

Small Farm Tractors

Once the size of your cultivated ground gets up to five or more acres, it's time to start thinking of equipment larger than that handled by garden tractors. You can go to new small farm tractors and equipment, but normally, that move will cost you more money than your five to twenty-five acres of homestead food-raising can justify. Far more practical, if you have any mechanical ability at all, is to shop around for used small farm tractors and equipment.

What you need is a tractor with horsepower from twenty to forty, a two-bottom plow, about an eight-foot disk, a spike-tooth harrow about nine feet wide, a two-row planter, and a two-row cultivator.

Believe it or not, it's possible to pay less for all this equipment to farm fifteen acres than for a new garden tractor and equipment to farm three acres. A tractor of about thirty HP, up to twenty years old, in good running order may cost you $500 or $1,000 (depending on its desirability at any given time), but even at the higher price you get much more for your money than you get for a $2,000 garden tractor. The hitch is that with the old farm tractor, you will probably be making repairs rather continuously.

Don't let that stop you. A good small farm tractor, unlike a smaller garden tractor, can be kept running almost indefinitely. I have one that's twenty-five years old and has had just about everything on it replaced at least once. I've painted it up and it looks like new. It cost me $300 plus about another $300 in repairs. It needs a new clutch right now, next year I should replace the radiator core, and a ring job for the poor old thing is a must next year too. But even with something to repair every year, I know I'm ahead of the game.

Buying a used tractor is as much a form of gambling as betting on horses. But you can cut the odds a little. Don't buy anything that can't be started and run— unless you like to restore old tractors. After the tractor motor has run a little, pull the oil dipstick out and take a look at the oil on it. If the color is milky gray, put the dipstick in the tractor, turn around, walk away, and do not look back. Milky gray oil means water is getting into the oil which means most likely a crack in the block.

However, if you are a mechanic (or want to become one in a hurry), remember that anything can be fixed, including a cracked block. If you point out to the owner of the tractor that there's water in the oil, he might knock $300 off what he has just told you was rock bottom price. That $300 would about pay for cold-welding the cracked block or replacing it with a sound block.

The older, small farm tractors are fairly easy to take apart and put back together again—at least compared to automobiles. If you do the taking apart and putting back together yourself, you can save about half the cost of getting a tractor repaired. If a farm implement company hauls your tractor into its shop, and its mechanics do all the work, you'll pay a lot more than if you tear the tractor down and haul the diseased block into a small independent (but honest) mechanic who can then devote all his time to doing the skilled work. He almost always charges at a lesser rate, too, because he has lower overhead.

A couple more tips to tractor hunters and would-be fixers. In every state I'm familiar with, there are used parts dealers scattered about who will have parts for many makes and models of old tractors. You won't have to ask many farm implement dealers before you find one who can tell you where there's such a parts depot near you. By the same token (sometimes it's the same place) you can find used farm machinery dealers who have old equipment to fit your old tractor.

Implements

Small farm tractors and equipment adapted to the three-point-hitch system, which allows you to mount, transport, and unmount equipment with great ease, are much more in demand than tractors without this system and the simple pull-type equipment they use. Therefore, three-point-hitch equipment will be invariably more expensive to buy—even used. In tractors equal in other respects, the difference may be as much as $400 or more. An old three-point-hitch plow may command fifty dollars, while a pull-type of the same size only fifteen dollars. A farmer *gave* me an old pull-type disk that I still use. Had it been adapted to three-point-hitch, I'd have paid fifty dollars for it. I think three-point-hitch equipment is worth it, but if you want to economize, you don't need it—especially if all your land is in one place and you don't have to move equipment over roads.

The two-row cultivator you'll need to cultivate weeds planted with a two-row planter can be the most difficult tool to find. Many old tractors are sold with the two-row cultivator that mounts on them. Get it if you can, or inquire where you can find one that fits the tractor you want to buy. The other alternative is to find a two-row cultivator that you simply pull with your tractor. These are hard to find as most old two-row cultivators mount partly on the front of the tractor and partly behind (and are devils to put on). If you can't find a cultivator that mounts easily and solely to the rear of your tractor, look for a four-row cultivator of this type. They are more common, but are already obsolete on commercial farms, so can be purchased reasonably. All you have to do is cut off the two outside gangs with a welding torch to make yourself a two-row cultivator. If you are asking yourself why you can't use a four-row cultivator to cultivate rows planted with a two-row planter, the answer is row spacing. No matter how good a tractor driver you fancy yourself, there are going to be variables in your two-row passes with the planter. You'll be closer to the already planted rows one time, a little farther away another time. The cultivator will not allow for these variables and, if you try to use a four-row cultivator to cultivate rows planted with a two-row planter, you'll probably rip up two rows with each pass.

One word of advice: when you buy your old tractor, you will be better off to buy a brand made by a company still active in making farm machinery. That includes John Deere, Ford, Massey-Ferguson, White (which includes Oliver), Allis Chalmers, and International Harvester. After you buy, be sure to order (through a local dealer) the parts and operating maintenance manuals for your specific tractor. In most cases, you can get them even for twenty-year-old tractors.

Good luck in your repair work. You'll need it. But a man's labor is almost always repaid. With rampant inflation and shortages, old tractors kept in good repair are selling today for more than their new price. That's almost *any* used tractor. Those with antique value have risen unbelievably in price. I know a fellow with a 1910 tractor in good running order who won't take $25,000 for it!

Notes

The Danger of Erosion

1. (p. 5) "Geological erosion tends to be static, for soil builds as fast or a little faster than water carries it away. Man-made erosion is dynamic and cumulative and has no end save complete destruction. Without erosion control, reservoirs will fill with silt, dams will become useless, power supplies will be shut off, floods will be increased in violence, irrigation projects will be ruined, navigation will be disrupted, wildlife will be progressively destroyed, recreation facilities will be increasingly limited. It is not a simple matter of growing food. Adequate calories might conceivably be secured by growing plants indoors in cabinets, as competent scientists have suggested. But if we neglect the soil on the score of the food supply alone, we expose ourselves to alarming deficiencies in other economic fields, to say nothing of destroying the surface on which after all, we must build our houses, carry on our work, and continue to live."

Stuart Chase, *Rich Land, Poor Land: A Study of Waste in the Natural Resources of America* (New York, AMS Press, 1969; first published 1936), p. 57.

Nitrogen and Phosphorus Fixation

2. (p. 47) "Agricultural prosperity of any region of the world could easily be traced to the fertility status of the soils of that region, which in turn reflects man's ability

222

to enrich the soil with extra quantities of nitrogen. The future of mankind on this planet therefore depends upon man's ability to find economic ways and means of fixing atmospheric nitrogen into soil, which would alone assure adequate supply of food material required for the survival of man and his domesticated animals. . . . In India about 24 million hectares of land is under pulses, fodder, and green manure legumes. It is roughly estimated that about .91 million tons of nitrogen is fixed by the *Rhizobium spp.* functioning in symbiosis with the legume roots. . . .

"Better understanding of the symbiotic relationships in the legumes and *Rhizobium spp.* would lead to studies on symbiotic nitrogen fixation in non-leguminous, annual crops like cereals, solanaceous vegetables, oilseed crops, etc. It has been suggested that when once the biochemical basis for infection, nodulation and symbiotic nitrogen fixation is known, we could supplement the non-leguminous host plants with the required chemicals to make them accept the symbiotic partner. We may also be able to breed a new strain or species of *Rhizobium* or synthesize a new genus of nitrogen-fixing bacterium capable of infecting non-leguminous plants. . . .

"Besides symbiotic nitrogen-fixing organisms, free-living microorganisms play an important role in fixing atmospheric nitrogen and balancing the nitrogen cycle in nature. . . . Of these bacteria, species of Azotobacter are common in various soils and of Beijerinckia are found mostly in acid soils. . . . It is necessary to evolve a fast-growing and highly efficient strain of Azotobacter which is capable of multiplying and fixing large quantities of nitrogen under various moisture and other physical and chemical stresses in the soil. Studies carried out so far have indicated the possibilities of modifying several physiological properties, including nitrogen-fixing efficiency of Azotobacter and concerted efforts would yield fruitful results.

"Recent studies on the physiological activities of rhizosphere microflora have shown that a few species of Azotobacter are present in the rhizospheres of several cereals and other non-legumes. Though their nitrogen-fixing quality *in situ* is not understood there are indirect evidences to show that their presence helps plant growth. Pre-treatment of the seed with strains of Azotobacter before sowing, dipping the roots of seedlings in a suspension of Azotobacter before transplanting and addition of the bacterial culture into the soil before and after transplanting has been found to benefit rice, ragi (*Pleusine coracana*) and tomato plants. The addition of the bacterium has been found to reduce the requirement of nitrogenous fertilizer by about 20 to 40 kg/ha. Mere pre-treatment of the seed with efficient strains of Azotobacter has been found to enhance seedling growth by about 10 to 20% and improve crop stand in the field. It is possible to improve the nitrogen-fixing quality of Azotobacter to make it competitive in not only establishing in plant rhizosphere but also in utilizing the spectrum of chemicals exuded by plant roots. . . . When such systems are perfected, it would be possible to substantially economize nitrogenous fertilizer requirement of non-leguminous crop plants. . . .

"Phosphobacteria present in free-living forms in soils are reported to help the plants through mobilization of insoluble forms of phosphates into soluble forms. Pretreatment of the seeds of cereals with Phosphobacteria has helped in reducing fertilizer phosphate requirement and increasing crop yields. The bacterium dissolves native phosphate through enzymatic action and makes it available for plant growth. Phosphobacteria are reported to be present in larger number in the rhizosphere regions of legume plants than in non-legumes. Crop rotations in which cereal crops follow legumes are known to derive double benefits by way of added nitrogen and soluble phosphate in the soil."

From a Report by G. Rangaswami, Vice-Chancellor,
Tamil Nadu Agricultural University,
Coimbatore, India

There Is No Synthetic Nitrogen

3. (p. 50) The best answer I've read as to whether "natural" nitrogen is better or worse than "chemical" nitrogen comes from J. I. Rodale : "In chemistry we deal with compounds—combinations of two or more elements, like nitrogen, oxygen, sulfur, etc. Water is a compound consisting of hydrogen and oxygen, and it can be broken down into its separate elements, the building blocks. At times we organic practitioners have let our enthusiasm run away with us, upsetting a few of the basic rules of chemistry. We have said that the nitrogen which is in organic matter is different from the nitrogen in a chemical fertilizer. But this is not so. Nitrogen is always nitrogen and phosphorus is always phosphorus. It is like saying that six is always six and eight is always eight. There can be no such thing as a synthetic nitrogen. Man cannot bring nitrogen into being.

"Protein is a different story. It consists of a maximum of 6 elements—carbon, hydrogen, oxygen, nitrogen, sulfur and phosphorus. There can be different proportions of each one of these 6. Mathematics can be so fantastic that it has been said that over 6 billion different combinations of these elements are known. In other words, there are over 6 billion different kinds of protein —so you can see that it is possible for a great variation and even for a bastard protein to creep in here and there. There are delicate relationships in the formation of compounds. For example, water is made up of two parts of hydrogen and one of oxygen. But in hydrogen peroxide the molecule is made up of the same two elements and yet it is a poison. It consists of two atoms of hydrogen and two of oxygen. Only one atom of oxygen more—and yet it can kill.

". . . Protein has no uniform formula, but varies according to how it originated. If it has an artificial chemical origin, it is entirely possible that the atoms may arrange themselves differently within the molecule than if the nitrogen is of organic origin. Nature has a way of arranging them based on an evolution of millions of years."

J. I. Rodale, "Lessons In Organics,"
in OGF, February 1967, pp. 131-132.

Fertility Influences Taste

4. (p. 50) The best wines contain the most phosphorus. A French chemist named Paturel has shown that when vintages of different years are arranged in order of P_2O_2 content, the sequence is almost identical with the order of excellence assigned by wine merchants."

Stuart Chase, Rich Land, Poor Land, p. 212.

Manure—Still An Efficient Fertilizer

5. (p. 51) "For the foreseeable future, I believe the mainstay of livestock waste management will be application of manure or treated effluents on or in the soil. Lately the energy crisis has converted a chronic problem of the feedlot industry—that of increasing manure accumulation—into the only profit source available in cattle feeding during the last 6 months. With few exceptions, the large manure stockpiles that were once the trademark of the Texas cattle feeding industry are rapidly disappearing in the path of a fertilizer shortage and an intensive industry-university educational campaign for farmers. If crop yields from feedlot waste utilization obtained from research can be realized in large scale farming, a long-term steady market for feedlot manure may be at hand."

John M. Sweeten, Agricultural Engineer,
Texas A & M, in *Compost Science,*
September-October 1974, p. 20.

Poor Soil, Poor Health

6. (p. 59) Dr. William A. Albrecht, world-known agronomist and Professor Emeritus of the Department of Soils of the University of Missouri, pointed directly at the underlying cause for mounting disease problems in livestock. In an article in *OGF* Dr. Albrecht warned: "Evidences of declining soil fertility are seen in the greater number of deficiency diseases among our farm animals. Veterinarians are constantly faced with increasing cases of strange animal ailments for which no specific body weakness or visible physiological cause can be found. Eye ailments, a tendency to blindness, bad gaits, rounded back lines, inferior condition, poor feeding progress, and even debility and death can be traced to deficiencies in animals' nutrition.

"Confined as they are, animals are limited in their feeding by the soil fertility of the farm. Supplements such as proteins contain too little of the minerals needed. And when animals protest by rooting up the very earth or climbing the fence in search of better forage, such actions are met by rings in the nose or cumbersome yokes about the neck. Human serfs have been prohibited in this country for about 100 years, but animal slaves can be seen on any trip throughout the country. Too often they are almost in a state of starvation because their master, the farm owner, neglects his soil fertility."

In England . . . the importance of soil and livestock food was reported nearly 30 years ago. The *Gardener's Chronicle* of April 11, 1942, carried this item:

"At Marsden Park in Surrey in 1939, the following

results from feeding trials were obtained. Poultry, pigs, horses and dairy cows were fed separately on a grain ration raised from fertile soil and compared with a similar one purchased in the open market. In all cases the results were similar. The animals not only throve better on the grain from fertile soil, but needed less—a saving of about 15 percent was obtained.

"Resistance to disease markedly increased. The infantile mortality in poultry fell from 40 percent to 4 percent. In pigs, troubles like scours disappeared. Mares and cows showed none of the troubles which often occur at birth."

J. I. Rodale, "Lessons In Organics,"
in *OGF*, March 1968, p. 107.

Importance of Sulfur

7. (p. 61) "When rock phosphate is composted with sulfur and manure, the sulfuric acid formed by biological oxidation makes the insoluble phosphate available. Plants may get more phosphate from poorly soluble phosphate materials when they are grown in the presence of microbes than when they are grown under sterile conditions. Sulfur applied to soils as a corrective for excessive sodium salinity is ineffective until it has been oxidized to sulphate by the soil flora."

Francis E. Clark, "Living Organisms in the Soil,"
in *Soils, The USDA Yearbook of Agriculture,*
1957, pp. 157-164.

Manure and Phosphate Help Each Other

8. (p. 61) Not only does the manure help make the phosphoric acid in the rock phosphate more available, but "manure is deficient in phosphoric oxide and requires supplements in order to get the full value of the nitrogen and the potassium," according to Myron S. Anderson, "Farm Manure," in *Soils, The USDA Yearbook of Agriculture,* 1957, p. 235.

Mulch Means More Potassium

9. (p. 64) "Research . . . shows that large amounts of available potassium are found underneath old straw mulches as compared with adjacent cultivated land. In the *Journal of the American Society of Agronomy* 30:438-9 (1938), I. W. Wander and J. H. Gourley show that where there had been a heavy mulch for 22 to 38 years in a pear orchard, upon which no potassium had been added other than that supplied by the mulch, available potassium was very high to a depth of from 24 to 32 inches . . . and yet the straw contains only one percent potassium."

J. I. Rodale, "Lessons In Organics,"
in *OGF*, September 1970, p. 111.

Magnesium Imbalance Can Kill

10. (p. 77) "Grass tetany also known as 'staggers' and hypomagnesemia is one of the increasingly serious nutritional/metabolic disorders afflicting grazing animals. It is primarily caused by a magnesium imbalance in the diet. Initial symptoms include an inability to flex the hind legs, which cause the animal to walk stiffly; nervousness, decreased appetite and a dull appearance. This is followed by muscular twitching of the face and ears, increased nervousness and diarrhea. Advance signs include violent tetanic contractions of the limbs and tail, convulsions and grating of the teeth, and finally possible collapse and death. . . .

"Short-term solutions include dusting pastures with magnesium oxide. . . . A spray of magnesium oxide-bentonite clay-water slurry that adheres to the foliage and affords grazing animals a continuous intake appears promising. . . . Use 'soft' Mg blocks . . . with free choice salt/steamed bonemeal 50:50. . . . Fertilize with a soluble Mg salt. . . . Use lower rates of potassium fertilizer. . . . Avoid heavy nitrogen applications. . . .

"Long term solutions include increasing the Mg by applying high Mg limestone or dolomite. . . . Magnesite applied on the soil surface or mixed with the soil may be more effective than dolomite. . . . Pastures can be renovated and seeded with Mg accumulator plants— such as red clover and tall fescue or with species that respond favorably to Mg fertilizations. Avoid feeding or grazing grass species such as timothy and smooth bromegrass, which are generally low in Mg, during periods when tetany may be a problem."

> C. F. Gross, "Managing Magnesium Deficient Soils to Prevent Grass Tetany," in *Plants, Animals, and Man, Proceedings of the 28th Annual Meeting of the Soil Conservation Society of America,* 1973, pp. 88-92.

Rain, The Poor Man's Manure

11. (p. 79) "Rain brings with it much in the way of free fertilizer. Nitrogen is washed down to the extent of about 5 or 6 pounds per acre yearly, and even falls on the soil on dry days, but to a much lesser extent. In some places, it was found that rain brought down as high as 20 pounds per acre annually. This nitrogen is in a form that is readily available to plants. Snow furnishes not only nitrogen but also phosphorus and other minerals. That is why it has been referred to as 'the poor man's manure.' . . .

"Sulphur is another valuable element that comes down with the rain. . . . Tests in Florida at a government experiment station showed that sulphur is absolutely necessary in connection with the growing of oranges. But at the end of the long pamphlet in which the entire details of this experiment were demonstrated, and the disastrous consequences of a shortage of this element shown, it was mentioned casually that the orange grower need not worry about the lack of sulphur because 'there is a sufficient quantity of it in the air which is washed into the earth every time it rains. This takes care of the earth's normal sulphur requirements.' "

J. I. Rodale, "Lessons in Organics," in *OGF*, April 1969, p. 100.

Top-Dressed Manure Lessens Erosion

12. (p. 87) "In an experiment at Zanesville, Ohio, runoff and soil loss were measured from two corn plots, one top-dressed with manure and one not, on a 12% slope of Muskingum Silt Loam. Erosive rainfall was heavy the first year of the experiment. Soil loss from the untreated plot from late June until harvest was 41 tons an acre. Soil loss from the plot top-dressed with manure was 1.4 tons per acre. Runoff loss of water from the top-dressed plot was less than half of that from the unmanured plot."

Myron S. Anderson, "Farm Manure," p. 231.

Humus Is Alive

13. (p. 87) "Humus is made up from a group of very complex organic compounds depending on the nature of the residues from which it is formed, on the conditions under which decomposition takes place, and on the extent to which the processes of decay have proceeded. Humus, therefore, cannot be exactly the same thing everywhere. It is bound to be a creature of circumstance. Moreover it is alive and teems with a vast range of microorganisms which derive most of their nutriment from this substratum. Humus in the natural state is dynamic, not static. From the point of view of agriculture, therefore, we are dealing not with simple dead matter like a sack of sulphate of ammonia, which can be analyzed and valued according to its chemical composition, but with a vast organic complex in which an important section of the farmer's invisible labor force—the organisms which carry on the work of the soil—is temporarily housed. . . .

"It is essential at this point to pay some attention to the many-sided properties of humus and to realize how profoundly it differs from a chemical manure. At the moment all over the world, field trials—based on mere nitrogen content—are in progress for comparing on the current crop, dressings of humus and various artificial manures. A mere glance at the properties of humus will show that such field trials are based on a fundamental misconception of what soil fertility implies and are misleading and therefore useless."

Sir Albert Howard, *An Agricultural Testament*
(Emmaus, Pa., Rodale Press and Oxford University Press, 1972;
originally published Oxford, 1943),
pp. 26-27.

Organic Matter Shelters Microorganisms From Pesticides

14. (p. 91) "Soil microorganisms also demonstrate varying degrees of resistance or susceptibility to pesticides depending on their ecological growth habits, whether in the soil, the rhizosphere, or the rhizoplane. With certain exceptions, organisms that exist relatively free in soil are more susceptible to various toxicants than those intimately associated with either dead organic debris or other living organisms, including higher plants. This phenomenon is referred to as 'organic shielding' (Garrett, 1956; Kreutzer, 1965)."

J. F. Parr, "Effects of Pesticides on Microorganisms
in Soil and Water" (Agricultural Research Service,
USDA, Baton Rouge, La.), in *Pesticides in Soil
and Water,* ed. Wayne D. Guenzi (Madison, Wis.:
Soil Science Society of America, 1974), pp. 315-340.

Organic Mulch Controls Nematodes

15. (p. 91) "Root-knot is a disease caused by nematode species of the genus *Meloidogyne* which stimulate cell development, resulting in enlargement of root systems and formation of root galls. Infested plants are paler in color, wilt more easily, and die early. All U.S. crop losses from parasitic nematodes are estimated at $1.6 billion annually. The yearly damage to vegetables alone is estimated at over $2.5 million.

"In an ARS-sponsored project, Indian scientists found that oil cake applied to fields 3 weeks before planting significantly reduced root-knot damage to vegetable crops. The oil cake was applied at a rate of 5,500 pounds per hectare (2.47 acres). Oil cakes are the organic concentrated residues resulting from the extraction of oil from seeds of legumes and other oilseed-bearing plants.

"Fewer nematode females, eggs, and larvae were found in the root tissues of plants growing in the amended soil than in the nonamended soil. Also the egg-laying capacity of the females was reduced by about 50 percent."

From *Agricultural Research Bulletin*
of the Agricultural Research Service,
USDA (Washington, D.C., October 1974), p. 17.

The Soil's Workers

16. (p. 91) "Soil bacteria are not distributed uniformly through the soil. They commonly occur in clumps or colonies of few to thousands of individual cells. Because bacteria depend largely on organic matter for their food, they occur most abundantly near organic residues. . . . Even within the plow layer, islands of activity can be expected wherever food material exists.

"One site of intensive microbial colonization is at the surface of plant roots. We usually think that plant roots are in contact with the soil solution or soil particles, but actually the roots and root hairs are almost fully coated by a film of microorganisms. . . .

"Actinomycetes are microscopic organisms that in many respects resemble the bacteria. Their individual cells are of about the same size in cross-section, but unlike the bacteria, the actinomycetes form long, thread-like, branched filaments. . . .

"The actinomycetes in most soils are only about one-tenth to one-fifth as numerous as the bacteria. Because their cells are much bigger, the total weight of actinomycetes in an acre-foot roughly equals the weight of the bacteria. . . .

"Numerically, the fungi are fewer in soil than the bacteria or the actinomycetes. They account for perhaps no more than 1% of the total census of the three groups. . . . In actual amount of cell substance, their total acre-weight roughly equals the combined acre-weight of the bacteria and the actinomycetes. . . .

"Fungi are important in decay because they can initiate decomposition and because they grow vigorously once they have gained a foothold. They can attack organic residues . . . whose moisture contents are too low to permit bacterial invasions."

Francis E. Clark, "Living Organisms
In the Soil," pp. 157-164.

Chemicals Can Upset
Soil Life Balance

17. (p. 92) ". . . [A]ctinomycetes are probably second only to bacteria in importance in maintaining a satisfactory biological balance in soil, largely because of their widespread ability to produce antibiotics. . . . Actinomycetes do well in dry situations of high organic matter and high temperature, conditions that might be produced with proper organic amendments during a fallow period." Kenneth F. Baker and R. James Cook, *Biological Control of Plant Pathogens* (San Francisco: W. H. Freeman & Co., 1975), pp. 177-178. I shall quote this book frequently, as it is an important work for organic gardeners. Baker is professor of plant pathology at Berkeley and Cook a research plant pathologist at the USDA Experiment Station there. Their main theme is that man through overuse of chemicals can alter the life of soil microorganisms detrimentally by destroying the

underground balance of nature. Summing up their own position at the end of their book, the authors say (p. 348) : "Man's attempt to feed his teeming multitudes frequently disturbs the delicate balance below ground, as well as above. His naive assaults on the subterranean biological network often result in his entrapment; in freeing himself from one strand he becomes entangled in others. Numerous fortuitous demonstrations have shown that agriculture can function within the ecological limits of the soil flora and fauna, and these examples man must study deeply and reflectively. Unable to win by annihilating all competitors below ground, as he can the animals and plants above, man must come at length to understand the effects of what he does and work with, rather than ignore, the established order of the earth."

Soil Achieves "Balance of Nature" Without Chemicals

18. (p. 92) Baker and Cook (see note 17) offer many examples to demonstrate how soil microorganisms in naturally fertilized soil of high organic matter content, undisturbed by killing chemicals, reach a "state of dynamic equilibrium" which is "quite stable and has, like the spider's web, remarkable resiliency because it is biologically buffered" (p. 347). In such an underground environment, "good" bacteria, fungi, and actinomycetes prevent disease organisms from establishing themselves in numbers sufficiently large to cause symptoms in plants. In this state of dynamic equilibrium, say Baker and Cook (pp. 181-182), "bacteria are generally effective as scavengers and are thus important in competition. . . . Actinomycetes are poor as scavengers and in competition, but are excellent antibiotics producers. Fungi are effective in competition . . . and hyperparasitism, and some effectively produce antibiotics. . . . [B]acteria are effective in the rhizosphere and . . . [all three] are effective on the organic debris or crop residues during the host-free periods."

Chemicals Suppress
Soil Microbe Activity

19. (p. 92) In fact, hard scientific evidence is emerging from sources other than organic horticulture that pesticides can adversely affect the microbiological environment of the soil. "A consensus of the earlier reviews is that most herbicides and insecticides can indeed destroy soil microorganisms or suppress their activities if applied at excessive rates. When applied at recommended rates, these chemicals seldom reach soil concentrations of more than 2 or 3 ppm, assuming uniform mixing to a depth of 15 cm (Fletcher, 1960). In the field, however, these chemicals are often applied foliarly and at least initially, are not evenly distributed through the plow depth, but rather in zones of relatively high concentration near the soil surface. Thus, concentrations may vary tremendously from one point to another. Depending on their solubility, the soil moisture content, and the extent of absorption, some zones may reach concentrations of 100 ppm or more (Kearney et al., 1965). . . .

"Soil fungicides and fumigants undoubtedly cause the most drastic alteration of the microbiological equilibrium. Unlike herbicides and insecticides, these chemicals are intentionally applied as antimicrobial agents, usually at much higher rates (often equivalent to 30 or 40 ppm), and exhibit various degrees of specificity toward soilborne plant pathogens, principally fungi and parasitic nematodes. Their action, however, is seldom limited to the pathogen. The overall effect is one of partial sterilization, resulting in marked quantitative and qualitative changes in the soil microflora, and months or even years may be required before a new equilibrium or climax population is reestablished (Warcup, 1957; Martin, 1966; Alexander, 1969). In the process, beneficial microorganisms may be adversely affected for extended periods." J. F. Parr, "Effects of Pesticides on Microorganisms in Soil and Water," pp. 315-316.

Not only pesticides, but chemical fertilizers are known to adversely affect beneficial soil microorganisms. The prime example is anhydrous ammonia, a good whiff of which can kill a man, or when injected into the soil, can kill microorganisms along both sides of the injector knives. How wide a band? It depends on the concentration of the application. Chemical farmers would rather not talk about the problem, if they are aware of it at all, and shrug off the possible detrimental effects with an argument like this: "Farmers often ask whether the ammonia kills desirable soil organisms. The answer is yes, but the damage is insignificant because the effect of high concentration near the point of release is only temporary and affects only about one-fifth of the plow layer in a 40-inch spacing and none of the subsoil. The pH at the point of discharge goes very high but when the temperature is favorable for the growth of nitrifying organisms, the pH will probably decline to the original pH or lower within two or three weeks." Samuel R. Aldrich and Earl R. Leng, *Modern Corn Production* (Cincinnati, Ohio, 1965), p. 89.

Benefits of Organic Matter Are Dynamic

20. (p. 93) "When either raw organic matter or what we term finished compost is put into the soil, decay begins to take place. If there were no decomposition, these substances would be of little value. As it decays, nitrogen and other substances are released, and when there is sufficient organic matter for a continuous process of decomposition to go on, it maintains a goodly stream of nitrogen coming from it. There is a dynamic quality—a movement from the organic matter—that is required if it is to be of any value. Were all the organic matter to be applied to the soil in the most advanced stages of decay, there would be no nitrogen available from this source.

"Professor Sidney B. Haskell, a Director of the Massachusetts Agricultural Experiment Station, in his book *Farm Fertility* (Harper) says: 'The benefit comes not so much from the character of the final product as from the process of decay taking place in the soil itself. Organic matter to be functional in the soil must decay in the soil; and the supply must be constantly renewed. Otherwise we either have a barren condition of the soil, brought about by too great a decay of this humus and failure to replace it, or an equally unfavorable condition in which the soil organic matter is dead and inert, like so much peat, or in extreme cases similar in its inertness to coal itself.' "

J. I. Rodale, "Lessons In Organics,"
in *OGF*, December 1966, p. 74.

Health Hazard
From Sludge Very Slight

21. (p. 99) "The disease-causing agents that may occur in sludge are a proper concern of health agencies. The present official attitude, supported by experience and research, is that anaerobically digested sludge is so low in pathogenic bacteria, viruses, and parasites that it can be safely applied on land without further treatment. Heat-dried, activated sludge or pasteurized sludge is also considered safe. Composted sludge is considered essentially equal to pasteurized sludge because the prolonged heat of composting also kills pathogens. Most disease agents do not multiply in sludge and gradually die off. There is some disagreement on how fast this die-off occurs and on when sludge-treated land is safe for growing vegetable crops for human consumption. At present, we would not recommend growing vegetable crops during the first year of sludge application unless the sludge is disinfected by pasteurization or composting. The health hazards are probably very slight, but why take the chance?"

J. D. Menzies, "Composition and Properties of Sewage Sludge," in *Plants, Animals, and Man, Proceedings of the Soil Conservation Society of America,* 1973, pp. 139-141.

Basalt—An Aid To Composting

22. (p. 173) "At the Institute of Bio-Dynamic Research in the town of Griesheim (Germany), I saw a few years' work in making compost with ground-up basalt rock which startled me.

"By using the basalt, mixed with clay, experimenters here were able to prevent the temperature of the heap from going above 120° F. Regularly-made compost will rise to 170° F.—a tremendous difference—which produces sufficient heat to kill off bacteria and enzymes and to destroy valuable nutrients, especially nitrogen. It is astonishing to see many compost heaps in two rows, all those in one being made with basalt powder and those in the other row without any. The ones without the basalt had been 'burned down' to a much lower height than the basalt heaps. By the prevention of so much heating there was very little dropping or compacting of the organic materials, but the decay was just as effective. In fact, the German government research men who visited this Institute were astonished at the darkness and quality of this basaltic compost. The basalt heaps also permitted earthworms to work in them and to multiply, because of the lessened heat, and perhaps also because of the minerals in the rock on which they thrived. There were thousands of them in each basalt heap, but relatively few in the others.

"Basalt is widely distributed in the U.S. . . .

"I wrote regarding basalt to Dr. W. D. Keller, professor of geology at the University of Missouri, and in his reply he stated, 'Basalt rock is about the best balanced rock I know of for supplying plant nutrients.

Therefore, I believe that powdered basalt with an illite rich clay mixed with organic matter should provide the best average, all-purpose plant food possible unless one would want to sweeten it up with a little extra phosphate rock.'

". . . In my opinion, a mixture of phosphate, potash and basalt rock powder would make the ideal mineral fertilizer."

J. I. Rodale, "Lessons in Organics,"
in *OGF,* June 1969, pp. 81-82.

Heavy Metals and Sludge

23. (p. 177) "All sewage sludges and wastewaters contain a wide variety of chemical elements. Of the metals in sludge, cadmium, lead, arsenic, mercury, boron, cobalt, chromium, copper, nickel and zinc are of primary concern.

"The effect of metals in wastes on plant growth is controlled by the chemical properties of the element and the soil, the plant, the amounts of metals applied and in some instances the compositional ratio of metals within the wastes. For example, most metals are much less soluble at pH 6.5 and above than at lower pH's. A soil metal content safe at pH 7 can easily be lethal to plants at pH 5.5. Other soil properties that influence the metal chemistry in soils and their subsequent availability to crops include the cation exchange capacity, the organic matter content, the iron and aluminum contents, and the phosphate content of the amended soil. For one or more of these reasons, the metals potentially most hazardous to plant growth are zinc, copper, and nickel. Wastes occasionally contain high boron concentrations that can be toxic to plants on some soils.

"Because of interactions among metals in the soil, some elemental deficiencies in plants may be induced by sludge applications. Zinc is known to interact with phosphorus and cadmium in the soil. High applications of phosphorus, for example, may induce a zinc deficiency.

High amounts of zinc seem to depress cadmium uptake by plants. Manganese deficiencies noted in snap beans after sludge applications may have been induced by iron or zinc.

"The research needs concerned with heavy metal content of sewage of sludge include the relationship of the metal concentrations to crop yields, crop quality and the metal composition of various plant parts, particularly the edible parts. Cadmium, copper and zinc in large amounts appear to have the greatest potential hazard for the food chain. Because copper and zinc are low in many human diets, some increase in plant uptake may be beneficial. However, if they occur in very high amounts, they can be harmful. We need some critical health studies concerning cadium and cadmium : zinc ratios in foods.

"The organic matter in sludge contains natural chelating agents that may prevent metals from being toxic. If sludge applications are discontinued, the chelates may decompose and metal toxicities may arise. Long-term research needs include studies of the reversion of metals to other chemical forms once sludge spreading is discontinued and the organic matter content of the soil declines."

W. E. Larson, C. E. Clapp, and R. H. Dowdy, "Research Efforts and Needs in Using Sewage Wastes on Land," in *Plants, Animals, and Man, Proceedings of the Soil Conservation Society of America*, 1973, pp. 142-147.

Green Manure Saves Plant Nutrients

24. (p. 180) "The time of turning green manure crops under is important. . . . Fall-turned crops may lose most of their nitrogen by leaching before the following crop utilize it. Soybeans turned into a sandy soil in Alabama in the fall lost 70% of the added nitrogen by leaching, but the loss was 38% when soybeans were turned in the spring.

"Cover crops prevent leaching of nitrogen and potassium and possibly other elements from soils. Studies throughout the United States have shown that losses from leaching are reduced greatly by soil cover—a matter of great importance when soils are light and sandy."

T. Hayden Rogers and Joel E. Giddens, "Green Manure and Cover Crops," in *Soils, The USDA Yearbook of Agriculture*, 1957, p. 254.

Green Manuring Controls Plant Disease

25. (p. 190) Baker and Cook, cited above, demonstrate the value of green manuring as biological control of plant pathogens, because the cover crops provide the organic amendments soil microbes need to proliferate, antagonistic to the pathogens. Plowing under rye, they note, has been a traditional way to control potato scab, and certain volatile substances released from legume tissue decay may actually trigger germination of disease spores, but prevent their growth—so they germinate and are quickly digested by soil microorganisms. The researchers also note that bean growers in the Salinas Valley of California observed that Fusarium root rot was much less severe or nearly absent if beans were preceded by a crop of barley. They reason that the barley straw incorporated into the soil immobilizes nitrogen needed by the pathogen for growth.

INDEX

Index

Index

Soil fertility, 226-227
Soil maps, 24-26
Soil moisture, 192-195
Soil profiles, 31-32
Soil pulverizer. See Cultipacker.
Soil temperature, 195
Soil testing, 37-43, 70
Soil textures, 32-34
Soil uses, 17
Soils, 12-45
    Black chernozem soil, 20
    Limestone-rich loam, 14-15, 125
    Loess, 20
    Marginal, 17
    Muck, 19
    Mushroom soil, 14
    Perfect garden soil, 24
    Pine barren sand, 12-13
    "Poor" soil, 27-28
    Prairie soils, 18, 20
    Reclaimed land, 17
    Red podzol soil, 13-14
    "Rich" soil, 27-28
    Rocky soils, 15-16
    Shale, 16
    Silt, 32-34
    Stripped land, 16-17
    Subsoil, 14, 35-37
    Tilth, 22, 86, 130
    Topsoil, 18
Soybeans, 188-189
Spade, 196, 197-198, 203, 208

Sulfates, 79
Sulfur, 78-79, 126, 228, 230
Sulfuric acid, 61, 228
Symbiotic relationship, 170, 181, 223-224

T

Technology, 5-9
Thermophilic stage, 154
Tobacco stems, 64, 143
Tractors, farm, 218-221
Tractors, garden, 207-218
    Implements for, 209-218
    Riding, 208-218
    Walking, 207
Tree bark, 176
Trees, 30, 127
Trench treatment, 134
Tryptophan, 72

U

USDA, 2

V

Velvetbean, 189
Vetch, 189

W

Ward, Hugh, 88
Weed control, 200-202, 214
Williams, Dr. Roger, 67-68

Z

Zinc, 70-73